Profit & Purpose

Profit & Purpose

How Social Innovation Is Transforming Business for Good

Kyle Westaway

WILEY

For general information on our other products and services or for technical support, please contact our Customer Care Department within the United States at (800) 762-2974, outside the United States at (317) 572-3993 or fax (317) 572-4002.

Wiley publishes in a variety of print and electronic formats and by print-on-demand. Some material included with standard print versions of this book may not be included in e-books or in print-on-demand. If this book refers to media such as a CD or DVD that is not included in the version you purchased, you may download this material at http://booksupport.wiley.com. For more information about Wiley products, visit www.wiley.com.

Library of Congress Cataloging-in-Publication Data:

Westaway, Kyle.
  Profit & purpose: how social innovation is transforming business for good/Kyle Westaway.
    1 online resource.
  Includes index.
  Description based on print version record and CIP data provided by publisher; resource not viewed.
    ISBN 978-1-118-70855-2 (ePub) — ISBN 978-1-118-70856-9 (Adobe PDF) —
ISBN 978-1-118-70861-3 (cloth) 1. Social entrepreneurship.   2. New business enterprises. I.   Title.
    HD60
    658.4'08—dc23   2014013895

Printed in the United States of America

10 9 8 7 6 5 4 3 2 1

Contents

Acknowledgments

None of us create in a vacuum. We are all products of our communities. I am profoundly grateful for my community. Without them, there's no chance this book would have been written.

Mom and Dad, I've never doubted that I was loved. That has given me the freedom and audacity to dream big. But you also instilled in me a strong work ethic (scrubbing floors, mowing lawns, etc.) that equipped me with the work ethic to make those dreams to come to fruition. Katharine, you live from an uncompromising sense of justice and challenge me to do the same. Kristen and David, your interest and support in my work have been unquestioning, even when I don't follow the traditional path. Karoline, you have taught me about the importance of getting the details right. You make me better.

To my friends: Sean, Blair, Malik, Stef, Phil, and Rich. Your friendship and support has allowed me to endure through the process, and your feedback has sharpened the concepts in this book.

I am convinced that the best way to learn about social entrepreneurship is by doing it. I'm so thankful for Jess, Anthony, Sean, Annie, P' Wen, and the rest of the Biographe team. I've grown and learned so much from working alongside you. To all my clients, you inspire me, motivate me, and teach me more than you'll ever know. I consider myself incredibly blessed to be able to wake up every day and advise brilliant people dead set on creating a better world. Your lessons are all over the pages of this book.

Suzanne, thank you for believing in me and teaching me how to teach. Dean Minow and Dean Claypoole, thank you for your support of the social entrepreneurship movement at HLS. My students give me hope for the future of this movement.

To my friends in Nairobi: John, Alan, Prina, Charlene, Chrissie, Patricia, Heidi, Matt, Grant, Adam, Emma, Will, Laura, Sham, Tristan, and countless others. You made Nairobi feel like home while I was so far from home. To the team at Artcaffe, thank you for letting me sit for hours sipping coffee while I was typing away. To Elvis: thanks for allowing me to walk in Memphis every Wednesday night.

A big thanks to Brendon for creating the brand, to Emily for tirelessly working with me to edit my thoughts into something readable, to Nadia for running my life across multiple time zones, to Isaac and his team for their transcription, and to everybody at Wiley that believed this book needed to be written.

Summit Series and Catalyst friends—especially my CVO North Star—thank you for teaching me to make no small plans. To my community at TGC—especially Jon and Michael—you continue to inspire me to work together toward the renewal of all things. On earth as it is in heaven.

Introduction

Fluorescent bulbs buzzed overhead in the second-story room on a small side street in the notorious Nana red light district of Bangkok. A handful of us sat on plastic chairs around a fold-out table. A mere four feet separated us, but a gulf of life experience lay between us.

My friend Sean and I were on one side of the table. Two young professionals from New York City, we had the good fortune of growing up in middle-class American suburbs. Our parents sat down for dinner with us every night and ensured we were well equipped to succeed in life. We both had the opportunity to attend great schools and pursue the careers of our choosing.

Four Thai women sat on the other side of the table. They grew up in extreme poverty in northeast Thailand and had little education. More often than not their parents weren't able to feed all the mouths in their families. With only a few years of education they were forced, coerced, or tricked into moving to Bangkok to work and send money back to their families.

Upon arriving in the capital they discovered that the work they left home for was not in the restaurants or shops, as they had been promised, but in the bars and brothels of Bangkok's red light districts. They were horrified when they realized their fates. They had suffered from the oppressive rule of the brothel owners, the nightly rapes, the stinging shame of social scorn, and the battering of abusive boyfriends. Their families had rejected them. By anyone's estimation, these women were victims.

But that's not how they saw themselves. They considered themselves survivors.

They were full of personality and their eyes sparkled when they laughed. They loved joking around, even across the language barrier. And as they told us their stories, they expressed hope. They were the most resilient and powerful women I've ever had the privilege of meeting. They were meeting with us because they had escaped the bars and brothels and they were determined to make the most of the rest of their lives.

They didn't want much from us. They certainly didn't want our pity, and they didn't want our guilt. They didn't even want our money. What they wanted was opportunity. They wanted skills. They wanted dignity and respect. Most of all they wanted jobs, so they could raise their children and provide a better future for them.

That was our mission. We were there in Bangkok to launch our fashion brand called Biographe, which would give these women on-the-job training so they would have the skills to take the next steps in their lives away from the bars and brothels.

Our meeting with them was four years in the making, during which time our anti-sex trafficking nonprofit, The Blind Project, had been on the ground listening and learning from established organizations in the region. The Blind Project, founded by three friends of mine—Liem, Anthony, and Chad—had invited me to join upon returning from their first trip to Southeast Asia.

As The Blind Project continued to take trips back to Southeast Asia, we witnessed firsthand the lives of those ravaged by the sex trade. We met women and children who had been trafficked, studied prevention programs, and even did some undercover filming inside brothels, recording young girls being sold for pocket change.

Throughout Southeast Asia, we kept encountering women who had either escaped or been rescued from the trade, but were struggling in the next phase of life. Too many of them drifted back into the trade because they couldn't earn enough money to feed their families.

This broke our hearts. It also got us thinking.

As we'd been observing and interviewing, we'd been raising money for nonprofits we learned were doing good work in helping these women. But these organizations were focused on the women's immediate needs, and it became clear that these were unsustainable solutions that weren't able to produce longer-term change in the women's lives. It also became clear that the women didn't want charity; they didn't want to be dependent upon others' generosity.

They wanted the opportunity to take ownership of their lives and provide for their families in a dignified manner.

The problem of the sex trade is horribly complex and tackling it whole cloth would have been overwhelming. But we thought if we focused on these specific women, we could find a way to empower them to take the steps to make better lives.

Our solution was to create Biographe—a premium, socially conscious fashion brand that employs and empowers survivors of the commercial sex trade. The business model is simple: Our team of professional designers in New York design high-end jewelry and apparel, the survivors produce it in Bangkok, we market and sell the clothes and then reinvest all of the profits back into initiatives for fighting the commercial sex trade. This is the power of social entrepreneurship, putting commerce to work to improve lives.

When we launched Biographe, we were just focusing on solving a specific problem. We simply knew we wanted to leverage market economics to solve the problem of creating work for these women.

We didn't really think about breaking the traditional barriers between for-profit and non-profit. We wanted to deliver a product to the consumer that they valued so that we could make a good profit margin, so we were for-profit. But the whole goal of the business was to empower these women, so we were also performing the work of a non-profit. Why did we have to be one of the other? We thought there should be a third way that reconciled the goals of profit and purpose.

We soon came to learn that Biographe was only one tiny venture in a groundswell of entrepreneurships merging the pursuit of profit with the passion for a cause. The movement is global and spans the gamut from tiny startups like ours to some of the biggest companies on the planet.

The name of this movement is social entrepreneurship. Social entrepreneurship is the application of innovative business models to create positive social or environmental impact. It's where the heart of Gandhi meets the mind of Henry Ford. Throughout this book, we'll use the terms social innovation and social enterprise interchangeably with social entrepreneurship, as they are different expressions of the same concept.

When I first heard the term *social entrepreneurship*, I was excited for a number of reasons. I loved the way it captured the idea of bringing about social change by applying the lessons of business. It was validating to know that we were not alone in our thinking about business as a solution to social problems. It was also inspiring to be part of an emerging movement that I so strongly believed in. I dove in and started reading everything I could get my hands on about the topic.

As we were building Biographe, I also launched Westaway & Co., a law firm focused exclusively on counseling social entrepreneurs. In addition, I have the honor of co-teaching a class on social entrepreneurship as a Lecturer on Law at Harvard Law School. My experience as a social entrepreneur at Biographe, counseling social entrepreneurs, including some featured in this book, at Westaway & Co., and teaching social entrepreneurship at Harvard Law School has taught me many lessons about both the pitfalls and best practices in building a social enterprise.

Unfortunately, Biographe did not reach the scale of success we had envisioned, and we have transitioned operations to our partners on the ground for local production. Our failure to hit the tipping point opened my eyes to the many distinctive challenges of social entrepreneurship. Failure, often times, is the best teacher.

All of this experience in the field of social entrepreneurship has caused me to ask one question:

What are the keys to creating a successful social enterprise?

This book is the answer to that question. It is informed from my personal experience as a social entrepreneur and the years of counseling social entrepreneurs, but draws from extensive research into social entrepreneurship, including in-depth interviews of some of the most innovative and successful founders, including Scott Harrison of Charity: Water, Charles Best of DonorsChoose.org, Matt Stinchcomb of Etsy, and Neil Blumenthal of Warby Parker. I am more than ever convinced of the particular strengths of combining an innovative business model with a social mission for tackling the most pressing problems. Indeed, social entrepreneurship could be the greatest chance we've got.

Some skepticism has been expressed about the practicality of truly pursuing both profit and purpose. The notion that a business enterprise must exist solely for the purpose of making a profit and a nonprofit is the only way to pursue a social purpose seems to some an immutable law. For-profit companies are driven by maximizing profit, and there's no place for social or environmental goals, other than some charitable contributions and perhaps a corporate social responsibility program. Non-profit organizations will necessarily be diverted from their social missions by any sort of profit motivation. If you want to make money you go into the corporate world, and if you want to make the world a better place you go into the non-profit sector. Or, so the conventional wisdom goes.

It's time to move past the simplistic caricature that running a business for profit will make a person a greedy automaton who cares only about getting rich and not about making the world a better place. It's also time to move past the view that if you're on a mission to do social good, you've got to take a vow of poverty, which is okay because at least you're compensated by the reward of making the world a better place.

This either-or thinking is outdated, yet we seem to cling to it the way fifteenth century Europeans clung to the idea that the world is flat.

This is not to say that creating an enterprise that pursues both profit and a social purpose isn't challenging. Getting the balance right is definitely a tough feat. But as I researched social entrepreneurship, I constantly sought to discover whether there are any keys to creating a successful blending of profit and purpose, and I observed again and again that successful founders of social enterprises shared a set of values and methodology in pursuing the mission. That's what this book is all about: building thriving organizations that optimize for profit and purpose.

The innovative people behind these organizations are unconstrained by the traditional thinking about business and philanthropy. Their enterprises are not defined by their tax status, but rather by the impact they are creating. I am convinced that social entrepreneurship is the best way forward in solving the worst social ills. Social enterprises offer the most promising way to move past the hobbling limitations of traditional market capitalism as well as those of both philanthropy and governmental aid.

MOVING BEYOND SHAREHOLDER VALUE

By and large, capitalism has been a positive force in the world. Throughout history, as market economics has spread across the globe, a rise in living standards has followed. However, growth has begun to slow down and the side effects of that growth are beginning to catch up to us.

Michael Jensen and William Meckling, two economists, published an article in 1976 entitled, *Theory of the Firm: Managerial Behaviour, Agency Costs and Ownership Structure*, which argued that the owners of companies were being taken advantage of by the managers and executives of corporations. It's been wildly popular among academics and business gurus and remains the most-cited academic article about business to this day. This article inspired a powerful movement for managers to focus on maximizing financial returns to shareholders, known as the duty to maximize shareholder value.

In the swanky Pierre Hotel on August 12, 1981, Jack Welch, the CEO of General Electric, stepped up to the microphone and delivered a speech called "Growing Fast in a Slow Growth Economy," where he laid out his theory that the purpose of the corporation is to generate the maximum possible returns to shareholders, taking the idea of shareholder maximization mainstream. Board directors, executives, corporate lawyers, and academics have all but unanimously embraced this argument, to such an extent that the prevailing view is that maximizing shareholder value is a legal duty. There is, in truth, little legal basis for this view point, as cogently discussed in Lynn Stout's seminal book on the topic *The Shareholder Value Myth*. But precisely because so many corporate decision makers and lawyers believe it to be true, it has become a practical truth.

Under the shareholder-maximization paradigm, businesses are judged by one simple metric, their stock price, which has famously led to the single-minded drive to boost profits in order to drive up stock prices, leading to damaging short-term, quarter-to-quarter decision making, the illness that David Blood and Al Gore of Generation Investment Management call *short-termism*. This narrow, short-term thinking has had many damaging effects.

In order to show quarterly balance sheet growth, companies sell off valuable assets, delay investment in equipment, and cut back R&D budgets, draining resources and slowing innovation in the process. They also engage in creative accounting to hit quarterly sales targets, and too many have been driven to leverage the corporation to the brink of financial ruin, which has led to waves of corporate scandals. In addition, hostile corporate raiders have targeted companies with lagging stock prices, most often breaking them up and selling off the parts. This has made a small group of people very wealthy at the expense of communities that have been devastated by mass layoffs.

It's become clear that shareholder value maximization is often simply creating a short-term boost in the balance sheet at the cost of more substantial long-term value creation. The pure drive toward meeting or beating quarterly earnings has resulted in environmental and societal disasters from the BP oil spill to sweatshops to massive fraud at Enron and set the wheels in motion for the global financial crisis of 2008. After the crisis, even Jack Welch admitted that he may have been wrong all those years earlier at the Pierre Hotel. He noted, "On the face of it, shareholder value is the dumbest idea in the world."

The shareholder wealth-maximization version of capitalism has driven short-term decision making that has negative social, environmental, and financial consequences.

MOVING BEYOND GIVING

Philanthropy can be traced back to the time of Socrates, but the modern foundations arose after the Civil War in the United States out of the combination of vast newfound wealth and dramatic social problems to address. The very same gilded-age tycoons who made their money through exploitation, collusion, and coercion became some of the biggest philanthropists, seeking to redeem themselves for practicing dirty business by building libraries, schools, and symphony halls. The rich western governments have done the same.

The colonization and exploitation of the developing world, through the extraction of resources, were justified in the name of progress. When the colonialists were faced with the devastating consequences for the exploited nations, aid programs were created, in part to assuage the guilt but also to exercise influence as the developing world gained independence. The result has been called the Charitable Industrial Complex.

William Easterly, a professor of economics at New York University who studies aid, used World Bank figures to calculate that it takes $3,521 to raise the income of one person in the developing world by $3.65 per year. Results like this would bankrupt any company in the private sector but are condoned in the social sector.

Take aid to Africa as a prime example. According to Dambisa Moyo, a former Goldman Sachs economist and the author of *Dead Aid*, over the past 60 years at least $1 trillion of development-related aid has been transferred from rich countries to Africa. Yet real per-capita income today is lower than it was in the 1970s, and more than 50 percent of the population—more than 350 million people—live on less than a dollar a day. That figure has nearly doubled in two decades.

It seems that not only has aid not had a significant positive impact on the development of the African continent, it may have had a negative impact. The key reason is that while aid may have a short-term positive effect, it often has unanticipated negative long-term consequences.

Say for instance, you are a corn farmer. You are barely able to feed your family on the corn you raise and you have a bit extra to sell at market, from which you buy all the other essentials for your family to live on and to pay school fees for your children. You are making ends meet, but barely. Then a western country donates boatloads of corn to your town. So, suddenly the price of corn is free. The crop that you were going to bring to market is now worthless. Not only have you lost your ability to buy short-term essentials, but your kids can't go to school and you can't invest in next year's crop.

Once the food aid dries up your usual customers come back to you, but you have no corn to sell them. Now both your family and theirs go hungry.

In addition to aid destroying small local economies, it has a negative impact on exports. When there is an influx of money into an economy—and much aid is in the form of cash—the currency exchange rate is driven up, wiping out much of the advantage the country may have had in the export markets. Aid also encourages corruption among national leaders, who skim off funds to secure their power through patronage or simply to enrich themselves. Finally, the constant inflows of aid create a cycle of dependency. Why work hard and take ownership of the future of your community or country if you can just get by living on handouts?

Peter Buffett, the philanthropist son of Warren Buffett, wrote in an op-ed for the *New York Times*,

> As more lives and communities are destroyed by the system that creates vast amounts of wealth for the few, the more heroic it sounds to "give back." It's what I would call "conscience laundering"—feeling better about accumulating more than any one person could possibly need to live on by sprinkling a little around as an act of charity.
>
> But this just keeps the existing structure of inequality in place. The rich sleep better at night, while others get just enough to keep the pot from boiling over. Nearly every time someone feels better by doing good, on the other side of the world (or street), someone else is further locked into a system that will not allow the true flourishing of his or her nature or the opportunity to live a joyful and fulfilled life.

This *conscience laundering* is not only for the extremely wealthy or big governments; it has hit the average U.S. citizen as well. The 1984 famine in Ethiopia hit our TV screens in a way that no other disaster had up to that point. It's not that famines like this haven't been happening since the dawn of man, it's just that this one famine was invading our living rooms. Pop stars rallied together to create the iconic (and slightly demeaning) pop single "Do They Know It's

Christmas" and the Live Aid concert, raising millions for relief. Charities saw that mass consumers were willing to open their wallets if they were moved, so they began airing more TV ads designed to play on our emotions, telling us that for just a few pennies a day we could sponsor a child and change his life. All the major charities started to employ this approach, and it became known as poverty porn.

One problem with these pleas is that people can become fatigued. Another problem with this kind of charitable giving is that there's been little accountability about where the money is going. Some reporters have dug into big charities to look into that and in a few cases revelations emerged about extreme waste, high administrative costs, and outright fraud. Those reports generated skepticism and have had a lasting impact on the psyches of potential donors. A recent survey by Bank of America noted that the top two impediments to giving are perceptions of inefficiency and a lack of transparency.

Many charitable organizations have no doubt done a great deal of good, but the fact is that even massive amounts of aid and charitable giving have been unable to solve many of the most pressing problems, from providing clean water to making sure all children get a good education and basic health care.

Albert Einstein once said, "We cannot solve our problems with the same thinking that created them." Corporate capitalism has for the most part chosen not to tackle these problems, and traditional philanthropy has fallen far short. We have to think differently.

A BETTER WAY FORWARD

An increasingly influential cadre of economists, corporate leaders, leaders in the non-profit sector, and founders of organizations are forging a better way. Management professor R. Edward Freeman introduced a powerful new concept to counter shareholder management called stakeholder management. Rather than judging success simply by the value the company is creating for shareholders, this approach puts forward a broader concept of value, which includes not only the shareholders but also the customers, community, employees, suppliers, and the environment—collectively know as stakeholders.

While traditional corporate accounting focuses on the single bottom line of profits, John Elkington, founder of SustainAbility—a think tank on sustainable business—devised a new way to measure the performance of a company called the triple bottom line. Triple bottom line accounting measures not only the financial performance but also the social and environmental performance of a company. These three bottom lines are often referred to as "people, profit, planet."

In 2011, Michael Porter and Mark Kramer introduced a new way to do business called Creating Shared Value (CSV). They established a framework to reinvent capitalism that would harness innovation as a means to both find new economic growth as well as solve social and environmental challenges by reconceiving products and markets, redefining value in the supply chain, and building supportive clusters of industry. CSV is starting to take hold across the business community, including Jack Welch's old company GE, which launched GE's Ecomagination line of products that had $18 billion in sales in 2009.

In addition, a growing number of organizations in the social sector are rejecting the guilt tactic and have shifted their focus to a relentless pursuit of more effective solutions, rejecting opacity and inefficiency and embracing innovative business models. They are seeking to develop better means of assisting communities by working more closely with them to diagnose the root causes of the problems and devise solutions, and they're engaging in rigorous measurement of their impact while operating with transparency and soliciting honest feedback.

What's more, the two streams of change are merging. While corporate capitalism is aspiring to more socially and environmentally responsible value creation, the social sector is incorporating lessons from successful business practices, and that rigor is driving higher impact.

CAN I REALLY DO WELL AND DO GOOD?

Some of you are probably skeptical. I don't blame you. I was, too. You may be asking, "Where's the data proving that the pursuit of profit and purpose can go together?" Let's take a look at some good data that can help us answer that question.

In his book *Firms of Endearment*, Raj Sisodia presents research on companies that embrace a multi-stakeholder approach to management. He selected 28 "Firms of Endearment"—18 publically traded and 10 private companies—purely on the criteria that they have embraced stakeholder value as their guiding principle for business strategy.

Like most of us, Sisodia's expectations for the financial performance of these companies were measured. It seems logical that a company will have to operate at slimmer margins if it wants to pay employees well, provide good healthcare, invest in the community, and operate in an environmentally friendly manner. But the findings of his study show otherwise.

Not only do the Firms of Endearment do social good, they also make their investors very happy. Between 1996 and 2011 the Firms of Endearment had a 20 percent annualized return on investment, as opposed to the S&P 500 that offered a 6.5 percent annualized return on investment in the same period. Firms of Endearment also weathered the financial crises much better than the S&P 500. So not only do the Firms of Endearment provide a better financial return, they also tend to be more resilient.

A 2014 study from the University of Northampton and the law firm Bates Wells Braithwaite also shows that social enterprises have more longevity than traditional private firms. It looks at survival rates of the top 100 social ventures in comparison with the FTSE—the top 100 companies by market capitalization on the London Stock Exchange—over a 30-year timeframe, from 1984 to 2014. The results of the study showed that social enterprises were slightly more likely to survive in the top list—41 percent of these social enterprises have endured, compared with 33 percent of the FTSE in that 30-year period.

There is some additional good evidence of the power of combining purpose with the pursuit of profit. An organization called Ethisphere has been measuring the ethical score of companies based on seven criteria: (1) strong internal ethical and compliance standards; (2) legal, regulatory, and reputational risk; (3) internal leadership; (4) industry leadership; (5) innovation contributing to the public wellbeing; (6) corporate citizenship and responsibility; and (7) corporate governance. The bottom line they've revealed is that high scorers tend to perform well financially. In 2011, 110 companies were identified as fitting the criteria, and the average of those companies' earnings outperformed the S&P 500 by 7.3 percent that year. They also enjoy higher brand reputation, higher customer loyalty, and lower turnover.

Finally, Daniel Pink in his book *Drive* attempts to answer the question of what motivates us to work. The research he cites shows that money matters to the extent that an employee feels like they are not taken advantage of, but once he or she is paid at a relatively fair wage, the primary motivations shift. He argues that there are three primary motivations to work: autonomy, mastery, and purpose. Autonomy is the ability to self-direct activities, not being micro-managed. Mastery is having the right amount of challenge to grow skills. Purpose is an ideal that the whole organization is working toward that transcends the pursuit of profit.

Social enterprises are the ideal place for autonomy, mastery, and purpose to flourish. Pink suggests that by engaging employees on all of these levels, they will work harder, be happier, and stay more engaged. If employees are happy, engaged, and working hard, it seems logical that a company will function in a healthy way internally as well as creating more inspired products and serving customers better. Such a company certainly seems like it would be a great place to work. Is it any surprise that financial performance would follow?

Fortune posts a list of the 100 best places to work every year, and that list consistently outperforms the S&P 500, with an annualized return of 10.81 percent as opposed to 4.49 percent for the S&P 500 from the years of 1997 to 2012. The cumulative stock market returns for the top 100 performed 366 percent higher than the S&P 500 over the same timeframe.

So the data seem to show that social enterprises perform very well. It's difficult to point to one exact reason for financial perform-ance. There are multiple factors at play in any single organization's financial performance. But one clear advantage is that an organiza-tion that has a more compelling story will need to spend less on marketing, and social enterprises, by definition, have a powerful fundamental message. An organization that has a stronger culture of innovation and collaboration will create better products that customers will love. An organization that treats customers with compassion and dignity will win their loyalty.

HOW SOCIAL ENTERPRISES ARE LEADING THE WAY

The strong evidence is that by working with the mind of Henry Ford and the heart of Gandhi, the founders and corporate leaders of these organizations are proving that for-profit businesses can be highly effective means for addressing intractable social ills, means that may well be more sustainable and ultimately have more impact than both philanthropic efforts and government aid.

This book profiles a number of the most successful pioneers of this new way forward, telling the stories of 13 organizations that range from non-profit to for-profit and hybrids of both, and from small startups to two multinational corporations with market capitalizations in the hundreds of billions.

Who are these social entrepreneurs?

BUILD

Rethinking how to encourage underperforming students in the urban United States to reach college in the most unlikely of ways, BUILD teaches them how to be entrepreneurs. Founded in East Palo Alto, BUILD is now in cities across the United States, working with local school systems to get students that otherwise would be dropping out of high school into college. BUILD has been recognized with the prestigious Ashoka Fellowship.

Burt's Bees

Coming out of the most unlikely of places—a roadside candle stand in rural Maine—for-profit Burt's Bees developed into a line of natural body care products. Their recognizable yellow packaging has become ubiquitous. After being acquired by Clorox for just shy of a billion dollars they have continued to grow while maintaining their purpose. Incidentally, they have been quite a positive influence on their new parent company.

Charity: Water

Nearly a billion people across the world lack access to clean drinking water. Charity: Water set out with the audacious goal of bringing that number to zero. Given their progress in less than a decade—raising hundreds of millions of dollars and digging wells across the world—they just might be able to do it.

D-Rev

Why is 100 percent of the design brainpower focused on making more stuff for the 10 percent richest people on the planet? Don't the poor deserve good design? The folks at D-Rev think so. That's why they've been designing and selling brilliantly designed medical products to those living on less than $4 per day. Their products are improving lives from India to Latin America and turning heads along the way. D-Rev was named one of *Fast Company's* most innovative companies.

DonorsChoose.Org

Public school teachers generally have to dig into their own pockets to fund any special projects in their classrooms—can you believe that? The educational funding system is broken. Donors-Choose.org has disrupted the system by allowing the general public to fund a classroom project. This web platform that started in the Bronx has scaled to every city in the United States and is completely financially sustainable.

Etsy

Etsy has created a village community marketplace online, where craftsmen can connect with consumers and have personal interaction. The Amazon of handcrafted goods is empowering craftspeople to make a living creating handmade products as well as empowering consumers to do so consciously. They have exploded in the last few years with 2012 annual sales of more than $850 million.

EKOCYCLE

How do you make recycling cool? That is the question that performer Will.I.Am and Coca-Cola asked each other. The outgrowth of that conversation was the unlikely collaboration between a pop star and a cola company to create EKOCYCLE, a brand that creates products from recycled plastic bottles. Partnering with brands like Adidas, Beats by Dre, and Levi's, they encourage conscious consumption of up-market goods—making sustainability fashionable.

Embrace

About 20 million premature or low-birth-weight babies are born globally every year. A fraction of these babies happen to be born into families in the rich western countries, but most are born in developing countries with little access to an incubator—a vital machine to keep the babies alive. The founders of Embrace reimagined a baby incubator that would serve the developing markets. The result was a simple, elegant incubator at 1 percent of the cost of traditional incubators, which is saving lives across India.

IBM

What does this stodgy old computer company have to do with changing the world? If you look closely, you might be surprised. IBM just launched the first commercial research lab for Africa, in Africa. They are focusing on creating commercially viable products that will address Africa's grand challenges. They built the technology that got man to the moon, can they build the next generation of technology to lift a continent out of poverty?

Method

Sometimes systemic change comes from the most unlikely places. Who would have thought that two twenty-something dudes who had trouble keeping their apartment clean could disrupt the cleaning aisle of the grocery store? That's Method's story, and their unique combination of style and natural ingredients launched their brand to hit the $100 million mark faster than many huge companies like Snapple, Ben & Jerry's, and Nike. The rest of the industry took notice that making sustainable products could make them a great deal of money, so all the big guys followed their lead into creating cleaning products that are better for the planet.

Nike

Since the sweatshop scandals of the 1990s, Nike has reinvented its paradigm for doing social good, moving beyond clichéd Corporate Social Responsibility to sustainable business innovation. Innovation throughout the design process has made Nike's products industry leading in terms of people and planet impact and they are making money doing it, with a market capitalization of $70 billion. The rest of the industry is racing to catch up.

Soma

Can a water filter change the world? Soma thinks so. The company has created a beautifully designed water carafe that filters water and looks amazing. But the real impact is unseen. Money from every carafe goes to fund clean water projects across the globe with Charity: Water. The company is also having positive environmental impact; it's created the world's first completely biodegradable filter. Soma was named one of *Fast Company's* most audacious companies.

Warby Parker

Why do eyeglasses—a 500-year-old technology—generally cost as much as an iPhone? Warby Parker believes it shouldn't be this way. It has disrupted the eye wear industry—playing David to Lexotica's Goliath—by offering super-stylish $95 glasses direct to the consumer on the Web. It must be doing something right because the company sold 500,000 pairs in the last few years and raised more than $100 million in venture capital funding. The company is poised to push into the mainstream. This success has been largely driven by its purpose to provide eyeglasses to the global poor in developing countries. For every pair the company sells, it distributes a pair to those in need, the one-for-one model.

Some of these organizations and their methods of achieving success are likely to be of more interest to you than others. Perhaps you're a brand manager at a huge consumer packaged goods (CPG) company, so you may be more naturally drawn toward the insights from Method, Burt's Bees, and EKOCYCLE. Maybe you're the founder of an innovative startup non-profit and you're especially interested in learning everything about the success of Charity: Water and DonorsChoose.org. You might be launching a new product and want to learn from the successes of Warby Parker and Soma. Or perhaps you work for a corporation and want to become a social intrapreneur, bringing the wisdom of these practices to your firm, so you want to understand how it was done at Nike and IBM. No matter your situation or special interests, I believe that each of the organizations profiled has valuable lessons for you.

WHAT SETS THESE SOCIAL ENTERPRISES APART?

I specifically selected the social enterprises profiled to span tax-status, geography, size, age, and industry in order to demonstrate that social entrepreneurship can be successful in any sector and at all levels.

The key question this book seeks to answer is what sets these successful organizations apart from so many others that have failed to take off? The bald truth is that there is no formula for success that emerges. Organizational development simply doesn't break down into neat formulas, and anyone should be skeptical about any lock-step guidelines. So, if you are looking for the secret sauce that will magically make you make billions while saving the world, sorry to disappoint.

What I will offer you is a core set of insights about the key phases you must be alert about in growing a social enterprise and the most important methods and ways of thinking during each that will give you the best chances of succeeding. Though the building of an organization is never a purely linear, step-by-step process, but rather one of fits and starts, mis-directions, and outright failures, I have found that there are in fact distinctive phases in the building process that all of the social enterprises I've studied went through. These phases might also be thought of as distinctive challenges, and success in each leans especially heavily on a particular characteristic of the manner in which the successful founders I've studied and interviewed went about the process.

That core set of phases breaks down into:

- Discover—Finding the right opportunity.
- Design—Crafting a prototype.
- Build—Building a product and an organization.
- Fund—Capitalizing the organization.
- Connect—Marketing the product.
- Scale—Rapidly growing the organization.
- Evaluate—Measuring performance.

This is of course by no means a hard and fast construct; the stages may, in fact, overlap. When does the designing stop and the building begin? Finding funding is often an ongoing process well through launch. And the phases may proceed in different ways for different organizations. For instance, the funding stage may have to happen before building if an expensive prototype is required. But the construct should help you to anticipate the challenges you'll face and their distinctive requirements.

In that regard, my interviews with all of the founders revealed a handful of key qualities and ways of thinking and operating that allowed them to succeed in the face of each of the particular challenges of the growth phases:

- Curiosity
- Humility
- Hustle
- Commitment

- Authenticity
- Community
- Honesty

Each of these is of course important all the way through the process, but just as in life there may be times we will profit especially from a certain characteristic, such as curiosity when we are in school, authenticity when we're dating, and commitment when we are married, it's also true that each of these characteristics is especially helpful during one of the stages of growing social enterprise. So I have organized the book to focus each chapter on the pairing of one of the phases of growth and one of these core qualities.

The chapters break down as follows:

- Discover through curiosity. Finding the right opportunity catalyzes impact.
- Design with humility. Prioritizing users creates game-changing products.
- Build through hustle. Rallying people creates critical momentum for launch.
- Fund by commitment. Aligning funders around a vision creates committed partners.
- Connect with authenticity. Authentic connection builds a movement.
- Scale through community. Focusing on culture ensures smart growth.
- Evaluate with honesty. Honest measurement ensures continual improvement.

BEHIND THE SCENES

Because I believe that there is no more powerful way to convey insights than through a good story, I've focused on getting the nitty-gritty details of how each of the founders faced each of the challenges and telling those stories with a fullness that I hope is both engaging and more helpful than the more abstract presentation of action steps offered in so many books for entrepreneurs. I've strived to take you behind the scenes, doing my best to ask the founders all the things you would have asked them about if you could sit down with them. I've also strived to present their stories about the struggles they encountered with unvarnished honesty. So, the book includes tales of bad decisions and embarrassing failures and how each of these founders coped with those setbacks. I believe that failure is the best teacher, and should be celebrated not shamed.

Each chapter covers the stories of a number of enterprises, so you can also make contrasts and comparisons among approaches and take away from the book the lessons you feel will be most applicable to your own enterprise and its distinctive challenges. I've opened each chapter with some simple insights about what each phase of growth requires, and I've closed each by pulling out core lessons from the stories told.

My hope is that if you are an aspiring social entrepreneur, the book inspires you to take action and get going with the discovery and building process, and that if you are engaged in the thick of the struggle, that it gives you valuable ideas for overcoming the challenges you're facing. There's nothing I'd like more than for this book to help you in your own journey, so that together we can build the movement of social entrepreneurship through both profit and purpose.

Profit & Purpose

CHAPTER ONE

Discover Through Curiosity

The genesis of creating a successful social enterprise is discovering the right opportunity for you, one that will allow you to tackle a problem effectively, with your particular talents and will create significant impact. This is a process of discovery that involves defining a purpose, targeting a specific problem to tackle, and determining the approach to take.

Defining a clear purpose is essential. Purpose acts as a fuel, driving momentum forward. It's also a compass, keeping an organization moving in the right direction. Purpose is what gets an entrepreneur up at 5:00 a.m. to get to work. It's the reason why a social enterprise will be able to hire and retain high-caliber talent and keep them engaged once they are there. Purpose will attract the right type of funders and it will inspire people to become brand advocates, spreading the word about you and your product or service to their network.

Passion, talent, timing, place, and people must line up for a social entrepreneur to find the idea that is right for him or her. When all of those elements align correctly, a founder has discovered what I call the *Purpose Point* for an organization: the point where a founder's passions and skills can be used to their optimal capacity for the greatest impact. This is the sweet spot that aspiring entrepreneurs must find for themselves. It is the place of strength from which a social innovator should move into the world.

So how does a social entrepreneur, or social intrapreneur, find this Purpose Point? Doing so can seem as challenging as trapping lightning in a bottle. With a seemingly endless supply of problems to tackle, how should an aspiring social entrepreneur decide which one to pursue and which ones to pass on? Is finding the Purpose Point just dumb luck, or are other factors at play?

Every social entrepreneur follows a unique path. For some of the founders profiled here, their Purpose Point was discovered in a powerful personal moment that allowed them to see clearly the problem they wanted to tackle and how they could apply their particular talents to solving it. For others, their path was more analytical—systemically weighing their options. Still others were in the midst of pursuing one thing they thought was their purpose only to find their more authentic purpose was something else.

The social entrepreneurs in this book started their journeys at various levels of knowledge about the problems they were tackling, and skills required to execute on their vision. They came from all walks of life. They include the young and old, students and business professionals, a club promoter living the high life and a drifter. They are male and female, and are from a range of ethnic backgrounds. They found their Purpose Points in the most unexpected places, from a concert in Costa Rica to a scummy pond in West Africa to the rough streets of a decaying city.

Finding your Purpose Point is not unlike finding love: everybody must also find it in his or her own way. It's a mix of head and heart, analysis and intuition, and sometimes just pure luck. But though there is no formula for finding your way, there is a set of core insights that emerges from the stories of many successful social enterprises, which boils down to a simple but powerful set of key steps to take:

1. Specify the problem
2. Leverage shifts in culture
3. Build around talent

IDENTIFYING THE PROBLEM OF EYEGLASSES

In October 2008, Dave Gilboa walked off a plane and did something many of us have done: he left something behind. In his case, it was his $600 pair of glasses, which he'd stowed in the back of the seat in front of his.

He was a student at the Wharton School of Business at the time, and back in the computer lab, he recounted this minor tragedy to a few new-found business school friends—Neil Blumenthal, Andy Hunt, and Jeff Raider—lamenting that he had to pony up another $600 for a new pair of glasses.

"Why is a product that's essentially made with a 500-year-old technology the same price as an iPhone?" Dave asked.

Neil knew it didn't need to be that way.

Learning at the ScoJo Foundation

Five years earlier, Neil, whose undergraduate degree was in international affairs, wanted to do some work in international development. Through a random introduction from a friend, he met an eye doctor, Dr. Jordan Kassalow, who had started the ScoJo Foundation to bring glasses to the poor across the globe. Kassalow invited Neil to help monitor his first pilot program in El Salvador.

The foundation works with local entrepreneurs in the developing world to help them sell ultra-low-cost glasses in underserved communities. By tapping a local work force, the foundation solves the difficult problem in so much of the developing world of the last mile of distribution to rural areas, while also creating much-needed jobs. The foundation also trains the sales recruits to give eye exams, thereby improving eye care. And the impact doesn't stop there. The jobs created provide the recruits with a sense of dignity as well as the means to invest in the health and education of their families, which has further positive ripple effects for the communities. It's a powerful model.

According to Dr. Kassalow, "There are over 700 million people who need eyeglasses. It became clear to us pretty quickly that unless we created a market-based solution to the problem, we would never be able to scale. That's why I chose a social entrepreneurial model."

It sounds so simple. But it took a lot of trial and error to fully execute the vision of the ScoJo Foundation. During its first pilot, the goal was to partner with a microfinance institution that would give very small loans to the entrepreneurs to enable them to buy an initial inventory of glasses from ScoJo. The entrepreneurs would then pay the micro finance institution back after they had made money from selling the glasses.

The first lesson was that this model was not going to work because it required the most vulnerable people in the equation—the new entrepreneurs—to bear the burden of the financial risk if the glasses didn't sell.

So ScoJo switched from a microfinance model to a microconsignment model, giving the entrepreneurs the glasses on a consignment basis. This way the entrepreneurs pay ScoJo as they sell the glasses, and if they fail to make sales, they simply return the glasses.

Upon returning from the pilot in El Salvador, Neil was hired to work for the foundation full time and was put in charge of rolling out their programs globally. He was essentially launching a new startup every 18 months across the globe.

What Are the Stars Wearing?

The most striking lesson Neil learned over time was that no matter who you are—whether rich or poor, from the East or the West—design matters.

The ScoJo team started doing careful analysis of the style of frames that were selling and the ones that weren't in each area. To do a better job of catering to demand, they began watching TV and paying close attention to what the Hollywood, Bollywood, and Nollywood stars were wearing. They also went to upscale eyewear shops to discover the styles that were most popular. They were in relentless pursuit of all the information that would help them to create a product their customers actually wanted.

But to do that they would need to develop their own relationships with designers and manufacturers. One of the board members of ScoJo was from Oliver Peoples, and he began to show Neil the ropes of eyeglass manufacturing in Asia, taking him to the big trade shows and on visits to factories. Little by little, Neil learned the production process, and it became clear that it doesn't necessarily cost anything extra to design and manufacture glasses that are stylish than it does to make those that aren't. It simply takes intentionality.

So ScoJo began designing its own glasses and working with manufacturers to create the styles that specific segments of the market wanted, at a price point that was reasonable.

The foundation eventually rebranded and became VisionSpring, continuing to do great work across the globe.

Is There a Better Way for the Glasses Industry to Operate?

After five years of bringing the model into communities all around the developing world, Neil had decided to attend Wharton. Neil shared his insights from his VisionSpring work, with his new friends at Wharton, and, as business students are want to do, the four friends began riffing. Jeff shared that he had a pair of glasses at home that were put together with duct tape, and had a hard time justifying the cost of buying expensive glasses as a full-time student. Apparently, the high cost of glasses wasn't a problem only in poor countries. Andy chimed in that maybe glasses could be sold online, which could help to reduce the cost. They cooked up an idea: Might they apply the lessons Neil had learned to disrupt the eyewear industry?

The next day the four friends met up at a pub. Over a few Yeunglings, they decided that they really wanted to give the idea a shot. They would launch a company that would produce stylish, low-cost glasses and sell them online through the mail in the United States, for a start. For every pair of glasses they sold, they would give one away to someone in the developing world, following the established one-for-one model. Passion, talent, timing, place, and people had lined up for them.

The four immediately sketched out the basic idea for a company that would indeed soon upend the eyewear business. They were successful in large part because they had done a good job of identifying a very specific problem to solve, focusing just on making stylish glasses at low cost; they recognized and capitalized on the cultural shift of growing consumer demand, at all levels of the economy, for well-designed products; and they built on the solid foundation of the knowledge Neil had learned and their collective business school training.

RECOGNIZING THE RIGHT PROBLEM FOR YOU

Many aspiring social entrepreneurship don't gain clarity about what they want to create until they have a first-hand experience of some particular tragedy that sparks their passion. Both Jane Chen, one of the founders of Embrace, and for Scott Harrison, the founder of Charity: Water were catalyzed by personal experience. But they each took very different routes to that "aha" experience. Their stories are both great cases of how circuitous the journey of discovery can be.

When eight-year-old Jane Chen saw that her lemonade stand sales were not meeting her projections, she did what any good entrepreneur would do. She pivoted. Instead of sitting behind a lemonade stand all day and hoping for customers to wander by, she decided to take the lemonade to the customer. Jane Chen went mobile. Door-to-door, neighbor-by-neighbor, Jane knocked and made her pitch. Her pivot worked. Jane saw the sales of her lemonade skyrocket.

Jane is a born entrepreneur, but that didn't seem to be in her cards. As with many immigrant parents, her dad wanted a different path for his daughter than his own. His dream was for her to grow up to be a doctor. He was so focused on that dream that he would ask her again and again "What is your name?" to which she had been taught to respond "Dr. Chen." Jane ended up going her own way, though, and getting a business degree, becoming a consultant. Nonetheless, she would go on to save the lives of people all around the world.

While she was working in consulting in Taiwan, Chen happened to read an article in the *New York Times* about the AIDS crisis in central China. She couldn't believe what she was reading. Sixty to eighty percent of adults were HIV positive. The infections were not due to drug use or promiscuous behavior but to the government's shoddy blood-donation system, which wasn't sanitary. People were being exposed to infected blood.

Chen became obsessed with the issue. She would try to find any information she could about the crisis. She would talk to colleagues at work about it and friends at cocktail parties. Eventually she felt she had to go see for herself. She made a few trips to the region and finally met up with a nonprofit working on the problem, helping to care for the AIDS victims and their children. She discovered the non-profit was only allowed to operate on a promise of complete confidentiality. If the government found out that the group was spreading any word about the issue, the work would be stopped.

Jane began volunteering with the group, and she found that she loved the work. Though her management-consulting job was challenging and interesting, she realized she didn't feel an authentic sense of purpose in it. She also found that her skills from consulting were tremendously helpful in the nonprofit sector. She was able to bring rigorous business expertise to the organization and contribute to its growth.

Before long, she decided she wanted to move fully into the nonprofit world so that she could leverage her skills to maximize her impact. When she was asked to come on full time at the nonprofit, as program manager, she took the leap. She felt she had found the perfect marriage of meaning and talent. In the next few years, the nonprofit made huge strides on the issue. Their programs to care for the AIDS patients and their families continued to grow, and they earned the respect of the government and were able, after a long series of meetings, to persuade the government to give them the authorization to put a program in place to not only care for the victims but provide free education for all their children.

The Real Challenge

Before she knew it, she was on a plane back to the United States to start her joint degree at two of the most prestigious schools in the nation: Harvard's Kennedy School to get her master's in public policy, and Stanford's Graduate School of Business for her MBA. During the summers at Harvard, she interned with the Clinton Foundation in Tanzania, where they were working to develop a nationwide AIDS strategy. Jane's job was to work with the lab technicians across the country to ensure proper testing.

On one particular visit out to the rural villages, as Jane was going through all of the questions on her survey with a technician, the woman abruptly walked out of the lab saying, "I'm hungry. I have no food. I need to eat." It turned out that she had biked 30 kilometers to get there. Jane began to realize that it's not until you fix all aspects of a problem that you have created a truly impactful solution. If the lab technicians are starving, the accuracy of lab results is at risk. If women are not empowered by having real earning potential, they aren't going to be able to convince their husbands to wear a condom. If a country has massive amounts of anti-retroviral drugs, but no way to distribute them, they are useless.

Back at Stanford Business School, when she spotted a class in the course catalog titled "Design for Extreme Affordability," she was intrigued and signed up. The class was comprised of 50 percent engineers and 50 percent business school students, and the students were broken into teams. Each team was assigned a specific problem to solve by designing a new product. The catch was that the product had to be affordable to those living on less than $1 a day. This is definitely not a simple design task.

Jane's team was given the challenge of designing a baby incubator at 1 percent of the cost of a traditional incubator. The team set about doing some research, and when they crunched the numbers, they discovered that there are 20 million premature and low-birth-weight babies born every year. They traveled to Nepal to see the problem firsthand in rural areas plagued by extreme poverty. The big "aha" moment for the team was when they realized that they were thinking about the challenge incorrectly. They didn't need to just create a low-cost baby incubator. The real challenge was to save babies. Reframing the challenge from building a product to saving babies' lives forced the team to think differently about their approach to the solution.

If they just wanted to create a low-cost baby incubator, they could have taken a traditional incubator and just stripped it down to make a simpler, more affordable version. But the problem with that approach was that traditional incubators require constant access to electricity and trained professionals to operate them. They are also incredibly expensive, and the places with high infant mortality rates are most often poor rural communities where electricity is non-existent or sporadic and there are no trained medical professionals. So the solution had to be simple enough for a new mother or midwife to operate. On top of that, with care often happening in the home, incubators must be portable, not the bulky machines hospitals use.

Jane and her team came up with the idea for the Embrace Warmer, a device similar to an infant sleeping bag, which is heated by a packet of a wax-like substance that can be easily heated and reheated. They believed that if they didn't try to turn the idea into a viable product, nobody would, and they went for it. As we'll see in the next chapter, they had lots of hard work ahead of them, but they'd come up with a great product idea to fill a pressing need and that they were a good team to tackle creating it. Jane had been mobilized by her experience with the AIDS crisis, however, she found her purpose not out in the field but through a graduate school assignment.

Success Without Purpose

Scott Harrison's journey to discovery was both similar and different. Scott grew up an average kid from a church-going family in an average New Jersey suburb. Like a modern day prodigal son, at 18 he grew his hair out and started partying. Then he moved to New York City to join a band They played a few gigs around the city, but it didn't take him long to realize that the guy booking their band was making more money than the band members. So when, after a year, the band broke up, he asked the booking agent if he could work with him, and he started a new career as a club promoter.

His first gig was at a rhythm and blues night at a club on 14th Street. Chakha Khan and Brian McKnight would sometimes stop by. It was a great gig for a 19-year-old. But Scott was at the bottom of the food chain in the New York club promoter scene, and he was hungry for more. So when one of his buddies bet that he couldn't get a job at a hot new club called Lotus, he went for it and somehow talked his way into the position. He was now a promoter at one of the hottest new clubs in the city.

Promoting came naturally to him, and he steadily climbed the ladder in the club scene. The next 10 years went by in a blur. Better clubs, prettier girls, and always chasing the next best party were his life. Eventually, he found himself at the top of the scene. On any given night there are eight night-club promoters running the biggest gigs in the city, and Scott and his partner were two of the eight. Scott was living some people's dream, being paid $8,000 per month by alcohol brands just to drink their product in public, dating models, and dining out on expensive comped dinners. But he wasn't fulfilled.

On an epic party trip to Puta Del Esta in Brazil, after the bottles and models and $1,000 fireworks, he got up in the morning and sat on the beach, hungover, reading a book called *The Pursuit of God* that his dad had sent him. Something awakened inside of him. He asked himself what kind of legacy he wanted to leave: would it be purposeful? He knew he didn't want to be 60 years old, divorced, and spending his time chasing after 20-year-old models. He hadn't prayed in years, but he decided to give it a shot and ask God for a way out of his unfulfilled life.

About six months later, he saw his chance to escape. He rented a car and took off on an uncharted trip, ending up in Maine. While on the trip, he made a deal with God and decided to devote a year of his life to doing volunteer service somewhere. From an Internet café, right then, he applied to all the big humanitarian organizations including World Vision, Samaritan's Purse, the Peace Corps, and Mercy Ships. But he was rejected from every single one of them, because what does a humanitarian organization need with a club promoter?

As his luck turned out, though, Mercy Ships, a hospital on a ship that sails from port to port to conduct medical operations for those in need, had a ship that was about to set sail from Germany that needed a photographer and, when they went back through their rejected applicants, they decided to give Scott a call. Even though he had no guarantee that they would take him, Scott booked the next flight to Germany to meet with them, and he convinced them that his heart was in the right place and got the position. Obviously one of his real talents is persuasion.

The ship was sailing to West Africa, where the team would spend the next eight months. The night before the ship was to disembark, Scott got completely wasted. He had picked up so many vices over the last decade—smoking two and half packs of Marlboro Reds a day, drinking heavily, drugs, gambling, pornography, strip clubs, you name it. He decided this was the last hurrah for all of that; he needed to go all in on this new stage in life and give all of that up. The next morning he walked up the gang plank embarking on a new life and leaving the old life behind.

Three days later, the ship docked in Benin, greeted by a stadium-sized crowd waiting for surgery. Many of the patients were stricken with grotesque tumors on their faces, which made a profound impression on Scott. The ship was staffed with amazing doctors, but they couldn't see all of the people needing surgery. Those in the most dire situations were operated on, but many were turned away.

The next stop in Liberia was more of the same. The country was in a shambles after a prolonged civil war, and there was one doctor for every 50,000 people, with no electricity or running water in many places.

Every port of call was in similarly dire circumstances. Scott took 50,000 snapshots of the suffering, and he started blogging about the experience, sending out mass emails to the huge list of New Yorkers he had put together from promoting.

The Spark Had Been Ignited

When he returned to New York, Scott was full of a new passion to help those in the developing world. But he was completely broke and had to crash on friend's couches, living off the $100 here and there that friends would give him. He even sold his cherished DVD collection and camera gear. Before long, he decided to dive back into the club life, but this time to spread awareness of the devastation he had witnessed.

Scott convinced a high-end Chelsea gallery to host a nine-day exhibit to feature his photographs from the trip, with the highlight being powerful before-and-after images of the patients operated on. He also came up with a fundraising idea to support Mercy Ships.

One of the Mercy Ships initiatives was to dig wells to provide clean water to villages, and Scott decided he would try to sell $20 bottles of water at the exhibition to contribute to the water project. He had no idea if anybody would buy them, but it turned out they would. In the nine days, the exhibition raised a total of $96,000, mostly from the sale of Scott's photographs, but $15,000 was from the sale of the water.

The Problem Comes Into Focus

After that success, he flew back for another mission with Mercy Ships. This time around, he made friends with the guy who was managing the water project. Scott visited villages in Liberia and was shocked to see people drinking filthy water from swamps. His eyes were opened to a horrible reality that over a billion people on the planet have no access to clean water.

Scott realized that this one guy digging wells was making a huge impact at a relatively low cost. Each well cost a few thousand dollars and would provide clean water for hundreds of people. The simplicity of the solution hit him hard. Was the problem this solvable?

As Scott continued with his blogging, photography, and videography, he started not only telling the story of the patients on the boat, but also the water story out in the villages, blasting his posts out to his large email list. Let's just say he got a mixed response. Some didn't want to hear about it and would send responses along the lines of "Take me off this list, I signed up for the Prada party, not the freaking tumor." But he also received responses like, "I'm sitting here at my desk at Chanel and I'm weeping reading this story and seeing the photos." Some people told him they were moved to take action themselves and start volunteering or giving money.

After Scott's second tour with Mercy Ships, he decided to commit himself to fighting the crushing life conditions of the developing world. At first he thought the organization he wanted to found would take on multiple issues, and that he'd just start with water, which is why the organization is called Charity: Water. The idea was that over time he would add other issues after the colon. But as all social entrepreneurs soon discover, tackling just one problem is more than enough challenge, and you can't try to tackle a problem in its entirety; you've got to tightly focus.

Both Jane Chen and Scott Harrison stumbled upon a specific problem that resonated with them in the most unexpected ways. Their first-hand exposure to suffering drove them to take action. Does this mean that you should volunteer for some overseas project yourself in order to discover your own problem? Maybe. It's one good way to go. But the "aha" moment can also come to people who've done no such prior work, and your problem doesn't have to involve saving lives to have a meaningful impact. Consider the very different story of how the founders of Etsy stumbled on their idea.

A NEW KIND OF MARKETPLACE

In 1999, Rob Kalin and Matt Stinchcomb lived together in an overcrowded Brooklyn apartment. Matt was in a band called the French Kicks, and to make a little extra money on the road he started screenprinting t-shirts for his band. Other bands started asking Matt where he got his t-shirts and he started getting orders from them to make their t-shirts too. That turned into a small business that Rob and Matt ran together. When he wasn't screenprinting, Rob was making handmade wooden computers. The two roommates loved to build stuff.

At one point, Rob was also a little behind on the rent and he found out his landlord needed a web site for one of his restaurants. Rob saw an opportunity. He offered to build his landlord a web site in exchange for the back rent. There was only one problem; Rob didn't know how to build web sites. But he thought it couldn't be that hard, right? So he bought a book on HTML and got to work.

While he was building the site, he wanted to figure out how to animate an image of flames (yes, that was cool in 1999). So he posted about it on a message board and met two programmers from New York University, Chris Maguire and Haim Schoppik. They hit it off and decided that building web sites was an easy way to make some cash, so they teamed up to create a web design firm.

One of their first sites was called Get Crafty, which they built for their professor's wife, who was really into crafts. Building the site taught Rob that there was a big community of people involved in making crafts. Everybody was making things, but nobody had a good place to sell this stuff. And so he had his "aha" moment. What about creating an online marketplace for makers? Chris, Haim, and he set to work.

In brainstorming about what to call the site, Rob's roommate Matt suggested, only half in jest, calling it handjob.com. They thought better of it, and instead the team decided on Etsy.com, which launched in the summer of 2005.

A couple months later, Rob asked Matt to join the company to do marketing, and Matt responded that he didn't know anything about marketing, (which should have been obvious from his proposed name for the company). Rob shot back, "It doesn't matter, just do what you do for the band but for the web site." Matt was tired of life on the road, and he was ready to get married, so he took the position.

The team also added a more technically proficient programmer, based in New Mexico, named Jared. Matt and Rob worked out of their apartment in Brooklyn, and Chris and Haim worked out of theirs in Jersey. The team's passion was to create a site to promote the creative class, like their friends that were making great stuff.

Since 2005, Etsy has become the destination for hand-crafted goods. What started in a Brooklyn apartment has grown to a platform that sold more than $1 billion of hand-crafted goods in 2013.

In all four stories told so far in this chapter, the discovery of the problem involved serendipity, but this is not always the case. If you have the desire to create a solution, you can also be more methodical in the pursuit of an idea. Just take the case of the methodical Method men.

METHOD TO THEIR MADNESS

Adam Lowry was a chemical engineer and climate researcher and Eric Ryan was an advertising account manager when the childhood friends came up with their business idea. Both bachelors in their 20s, they were sharing an apartment in San Francisco. They had trouble keeping their apartment clean and were the last guys you'd expect to start a cleaning-products company.

But Adam and Eric were both looking to make a career change. As much as Adam loved doing research for the Kyoto Protocols, it was clear that he was just preaching to the choir of those who already cared about the environment. As for Eric, he was creating campaigns to sell stuff that he didn't care about. They were both looking for more purpose in their work.

Adam really wanted to find a way to reach people not already mobilized in the environmental movement, and he had come to believe that the way to do so would be to move from the policy world into business. In his world, business was seen as the enemy of the environment, but he was convinced it could be a powerful friend of the environment. He had determined to start a social enterprise to make some kind of pro-environment product, but he had no idea what the product should be.

Eric was interested in finding work he felt was more meaningful, and he liked the idea of starting a business with Adam, but he didn't know what it should be either. What they did know was that they wanted to create something that had both style and substance, that was fresh and also stood for something important. Instead of wracking their brains to come up with an idea for an innovative new product that the world had never seen, they decided that it might be easier to identify an established product that they could make more environmentally safe and also more stylish.

What was especially smart about their approach was that they made great use of leveraging not just one, but two powerful cultural shifts that were under way.

They harnessed the power of consumers' growing desire to buy lifestyle products that make a statement about who they are. And they capitalized on the still-building momentum behind consumer demand for environmentally friendly products. They also had a clear understanding of the innovation they would need to bring to the table—they knew that whatever their product was, it would have to make a significant step forward in the green movement.

By brainstorming for many hours one day, they hit on the category they would target. The desire for more stylish products was probably nowhere more evident than in the home. From coffee makers to closet organizers, product design had gone upscale, but they realized this trend hadn't yet come to cleaning products. This was a huge category, ruled by long-established brands, but they believed they had identified a gap in the market. Most cleaning products were still made of toxic chemicals, and the packaging had no hint of style. The big brands had missed the big cultural shifts that the two would leverage.

The idea would also build on their combined talents. Adam knew enough about chemistry to take the lead in product development and testing and Eric had design and marketing expertise from his work in advertising. When they thoroughly assessed the competition, they determined that nobody was doing what they had in mind, at least not well. The environmentally friendly products didn't work as well as those with the toxic chemicals, and no one's packaging really stood out for its design. Shopping for soap was like dating in a town with two options: Hire a so-called professional (a sure thing, even if it leaves you feeling dirty) or get stuck with a prude (and embrace austerity in the name of moral righteousness). They decided they would create a third option, a product that was natural and got the job done, and that looked great too—so great that even consumers with no particular interest in the green movement would want to buy. They would bring green to mainstream by making a desirable product that happened to be more sustainable.

They had absolutely no natural passion for cleaning products. But they had done a good job of identifying a specific problem, they realized how they could tap into the power of shifting consumer sentiment, and they drew on their combined strengths. Actually creating a successful product line and growing their market was by no means just a given, as we'll see in the next chapter, it took lots of persistence. But their methodical analysis had in fact uncovered a gap in the market, and within 14 years, the company had grown to more than $100 million in annual revenue.

The Method story is a great example of strategic product innovation drawing on considerable expertise. The design of the products is truly world class, and in-depth knowledge of chemistry was required. But founders don't have to take such a research-based approach to be able to build a large market. The story of Burt's Bees is a study in contrast.

INSPIRATION AT A SLEEPY ROADSIDE STAND

One summer day in 1984, Roxanne Quimby's life changed when her beat-up VW bus broke down on her way home in her small town in northern Maine. She put out her thumb to hitch a ride, and the gnarly looking man with long hair and big beard known to all in town as "Dirty Burt" happened to be driving by and picked her up.

Burt lived in an 8-foot by 8-foot turkey coop and had 50 beehives on his property. He would put the honey in old pickle jars and sell it at an old roadside stand where he would put out a money jar next to the honey for patrons to pay, then promptly set up his lawn chair and take a nap. Burt and Roxanne began to spend more time together. As Roxanne got to know Burt better, she realized that she might be able to add some value to his business. Of course, if Burt were just awake at his stand that would be an improvement, but Roxanne had a specific idea for product enhancement. She had an art degree and thought that they might be able to sell more honey if they improved the packaging. It worked; people bought more honey.

Roxanne then started making candles with the beeswax. So, they struck a deal: Burt would keep the bees and Roxanne would package the honey and make the candles. Sales of honey picked up and the candles were a hit.

They then began selling their products at craft fairs across the northeast, earning $200 at their first fair and $20,000 total in sales for their first year. That was not exactly a living, but their sales grew steadily from there. A few New York boutiques had seen the candles at regional craft fairs, so they began to carry the candles, and sales skyrocketed. So, Roxanne began to experiment with other products based on beeswax, formulating shoe and furniture polish as well as lip balm on the wood-burning stove in her cabin.

She also kept experimenting with the packaging and eventually ran into an artist at a craft fair who made wood-cut etchings. She commissioned an etching of a burly, bearded Burt, and they used it for their small tins of lip balm. The customers responded. The combination of the natural products on the inside and the vintage etching packaging gave them a distinctive brand identity. At the craft fairs they couldn't keep the lip balm in stock; its sales far eclipsed those of the polishes and candles. Roxanne took her cue from the customers and started to make other natural personal care products. These new products sold so well that eventually she stopped making candles and polishes altogether.

Roxanne didn't set out to create a company of any sort. She just stumbled into it. Burt and she caught the rising wave of consumer interest in natural products at that time, and she drew on her artistic talents to create brand imagery that connected powerfully with their niche target market. Roxanne discovered she had real talent for product development and marketing, and in 1999, she made a deal with Burt to buy his stake in the company and continued building it successfully. In 2007, the company was sold to Clorox for $931 million, generating some criticism in the environmental and natural goods community. But there is no denying that the Burt's Bees brand was one of the companies, along with Ben & Jerry's and Tom's of Maine, that helped to move the demand for natural products closer to the mainstream.

So much in growing a successful enterprise of any kind has to do with timing and with the speed at which the company attempts to scale. Burt's Bees is a good model for pursuing modest, incremental growth while continuously developing your product offerings and your business expertise. You don't have to "go big fast," as has been a mantra in Silicon Valley, and you don't have to invent a bold new product. If you identify a good product or service to offer, you can pursue a niche market if you are attuned to that market's desires.

INNOVATION FROM WITHIN

Discovering your purpose point can happen anywhere, including inside a big corporation. Social innovation isn't only for social entrepreneurs, those building organizations that change the world, it's just as relevant for social intrapreneurs, those launching innovative initiatives inside established corporations. Social intrapreneurship is powerful because of the scale of impact that is possible within a company with large budgets, extensive distribution channels, and existing relationships with customers.

Waste Is Only Waste If You Waste It

When Bea Perez received a call from her friend, she wasn't expecting to find herself backstage at an arena with one of the biggest pop stars on earth that evening. Sometimes really innovative opportunities come out of the blue.

Bea's friend said, "Will.I.Am would like to talk to you about an idea he has." She replied, "Okay, so when will that be?" He responded, "Tonight. He's in town for a concert. We'd love to have you backstage to talk about his idea."

She sat down with Will.I.Am. At that point Bea was in marketing at The Coca-Cola Company, so she was expecting to hear a marketing or endorsement pitch from the musician. Will.I.Am started with a story about a concert in Costa Rica. The concert was huge, about 100,000 people in attendance. Typically, as soon as the show ends the stars jump in vehicles and are whisked away from the venue back to their hotel in order to avoid traffic. That night they missed their cue and had to stay in the arena until the traffic thinned out. So, they decided to make the most of it and had their own little party at the venue. Little did Will.I.Am know that one missed cue would inspire a game-changing idea.

"We went out on the stage and we saw the aftermath of our concert. And the venue was just littered with trash—mostly bottles. Recycling bins were right next to the exits, so it isn't like people couldn't have just put the bottles in a bin. That was the first time that I realized that, wait a second here, our concert caused this much freaking waste? We played a big a role in this. I'm partially to blame," Will.I.Am said. "We bring people together with no culture other than consumption: eat, dance, drink, trash. So the physical manifestation of that was bottles, and trash, and cups. We wasted an opportunity to make something out of bringing people together. We left no message. We left no discipline, no tools. We left a big void."

He pitched a vision for products that are composed of recycled Coca-Cola bottles. He talked about getting other brands involved to make recycling cool, by creating aspirational goods that people would want. They would use the goods almost to create a whole new dialogue. He reasoned that if consumers knew how many bottles were inside that really cool jacket or iPhone case or jeans, maybe they would be more willing to recycle because then it would have value. To his thinking, waste is only waste if you waste it.

He tied the concept into Coca-Cola's goals for recycling, and made the case for a partnership that would help accelerate both of their goals for sustainability. In addition to achieving Coke's goals of increasing recycling rates of their packaging, a partnership could change manufacturing processes of the brands they work with and, perhaps most importantly, give consumers an opportunity for conscious consumption. Finally, they could use the profits for purpose by supporting grassroots community organizations that are promoting more sustainable living.

"You have to start conscious consumption somewhere, and an easy place to start is: 'when I buy this, it could turn into that,'" he said. "When I buy a Coke, let me make sure that after I buy this, I put it in a recycling bin to make it easier for it to turn into products I love." His concept was a virtuous cycle of recapturing waste and turning it into aspirational products, which encourage capturing more waste.

He called this partnership EKOCYCLE. A clever name, as the first four letters "EKOC" is an anagram of the word "COKE", and cycle refers to this virtuous cycle created by recycling and conscious consumption.

Will.I.Am really understood the goals and commitment of Coca-Cola. He'd done his homework on Coke's business and on the industry as a whole. He didn't have a naive idealistic pie-in-the-sky idea. Bea said, "He had a clear understanding of the challenges ahead of him. But he also had the passion and desire to give his own personal time and commitment to be a part of the solution. That's the same philosophy that Coca-Cola has. So our philosophies matched." Bea championed the EKOCYCLE internally, and after a few meetings was able to get approval for this innovative project.

THE BUMPY PATH TO INNOVATION

In the 1990s, Nike was in the headlines for all the wrong reasons. It was one of the first brands to be hit with accusations of poor working conditions at their factories in Asia

Their factories had a litany of worker rights' violations, including low wages, workers being fired for getting pregnant, workers being fired for trying to improve working conditions, and harsh punishments for underperformance such as licking the floor or being slapped with the sole of a shoe.

At the time the company was an adolescent, 20 years old as the scandal started to break. So, unsurprisingly, the reaction was very adolescent. Nike's stance was very defensive and aggressive. At first, they didn't own up to the problem. That denial and defensive stage was counterproductive, fueling the fire that began to rage against them.

It took five years before the leadership at Nike took a hard look at the reality and realized that the world was changing. The expectations of business were shifting underneath them, and they had missed the changes. Companies were just beginning to be held to higher standards—socially and environmentally. They realized that they were going to have to change. They had missed the weak signals. They missed the changing expectations for increased transparency, and they had to fundamentally rethink their approach to the issues.

Companies are made up of people. And, just as it is sometimes difficult for people to recognize that they need to change, companies struggle with the same thing. But the ones that don't change quickly become obsolete. (Think Kodak missing the digital photography revolution.) Nike decided to look inside, to pivot, to understand the cultural shift, and to accept it.

Nike pivoted from a stance of denial and defensiveness to one that engaged its critics, and started the journey toward change by creating a department of Corporate Social Responsibility (CSR). What followed was a lengthy year-long process of engaging with stakeholders, rethinking policy, and working on the ground.

But as they went through this process, the company realized two things. First, you need to go back in the business model and really try to understand what needs to change in the business to drive the behavior and the change on the ground. The second thing you learn is that you can't do it on your own, that you are going to need a massive new competency in collaboration across an industry that is profoundly competitive. You will also have multi-stakeholder coalitions and need to bring all of these parties together. So, Nike spent a great deal of time collaborating with external stakeholders.

Additionally, the CSR team was also looking internally. They started to look at the business model itself, asking a simple question: How do you integrate sustainability into the everyday fiber of the company? The search for the answer to that question forced them to look deeply and broadly. Fortunately, the team has a unique view across the entire company.

Nike's sustainability and innovation journey was established to hedge risk—the risk of bad publicity and damage to the goodwill of the brand. But it didn't end there. You may be surprised at how this journey completely transformed a $68 billion company.

AFRICA'S MOONSHOT

1911 was the year IBM was founded, the Model-Ts mingled with horse-drawn carriages on Main Street U.S.A., and bi-planes were in the air; the world had not yet experienced what would come to be called World War I and the United States was not yet suffering through prohibition.

Through the years, IBM has been a leading force in modern corporate America and contributed some of the most important advances in information technology. Their technology helped put a man on the moon, they were on the leading edge of both the super computer and the personal computer, and in 2011, IBM's Watson computer won the TV game show Jeopardy!.

All of these breakthroughs, from punch cards to vacuum tubes to machine learning and speech recognition, started in a research lab. IBM is a company built on the science and technology emerging from its labs, and those labs are known as some of the most prestigious research facilities in the world, packed with PhDs who are at the top of their field methodically working to develop the next generation of technology.

In the mid 1990s, IBM Research wanted to bring the research process to the global emerging markets in order to work with local teams on innovation, so they opened research facilities in China, India, and Brazil.

After the turn of the millennium, IBM Research Senior Vice President John Kelly challenged the division to move where the challenges are the hardest. The hardest, most intractable challenges the world is facing right now are on the continent of Africa.

The continent has great potential, with sub-Saharan Africa poised to have the most rapid population growth over the next 50 years. Africa has 60 percent of the world's uncultivated arable land. In 2008, Africa's consumer spending was more than Russia and India combined at $860 billion, and is projected to rise to $1.4 trillion by 2020. Fifty-two cities in Africa have more than 1 million people, more than Europe or North America, and 400 million Africans live in cities. Mobile phone subscribers doubled from 2000 to 2010, going from 300 to 600 million subscribers. By 2040, the continent will have a labor force of 1.1 billion people, more than China or India.

But it also has challenges that make it difficult to conduct business or research. The challenges include weak government, corruption, political instability, minimal infrastructure, and terrorism, just to name a few. These challenges can make it difficult for an established company to risk investing a significant amount of money in the continent.

IBM had already begun working with commercial clients in East Africa, but there was a real desire to do more. Internally, the question was posed among senior management "What is the best thing we can do to help the growth of Africa?" Other than the obvious answer of working with enterprises on the continent, which they were already doing, was there something more?

Given that over its century-long history, IBM had only established 12 labs, their CEO felt that the most precious gift they could give to the continent was a research lab. He saw it as a signal that they were serious about Africa. IBM was not just there to capitalize on the growth, but at the same time to contribute to solving some of the continent's most critical challenges.

That sparked internal debate on whether IBM could do it, and if now would be the right time. The head of research for growth markets, Robert Morris, eventually stepped up and said, "We cannot wait. This is where the hardest challenges are. So, we need to be here. We need to bring people here. We need to make a difference."

So, they started laying out the groundwork to build the first research lab in Africa. The first hire was the Lab Director, Dr. Kamal Bhattacharya—an IBM Distinguished Engineer with almost 15 years of IBM experience in roles focused on business and IT transformation in Europe, the United States, Asia, and Africa. Before being selected to head up the lab in Africa, Kamal was the Senior Manager at IBM Research—India, Bangalore, and, prior to that, team leader at Watson Research in New York, exploring new ideas in the area of IT Optimization.

Dr. Bhattacharya believes that Africa's unique challenges and constraints allow for the acceleration of scientific and technical innovations. As far as commercial and industrial development, though there are pockets of great advancement, much of the continent is far behind the western world. Dependency on aid, trade barriers, and an underdeveloped manufacturing industry have much of the continent living off subsistence farming in the manner Europe did prior to the industrial revolution.

With the rapid growth on the continent, Dr. Bhattacharya believes, in order to survive large leaps forward are required. "If you look at the downside of all this, population growth and urbanization, you could estimate that, from an agricultural and food security perspective, we need to accomplish in 20 to 30 years what it took Europe 200 years to accomplish."

IBM created the technology to get a man on the moon. Addressing the grand challenges of Africa is our generation's moonshot. It will require just as much creativity and innovation, and, if successful has the power to change the trajectory of an entire continent. IBM just launched the first private research facility in sub-Saharan Africa.

Dr. Bhattacharya says, "We just took the plunge. We don't know if that is the right thing to do, but it just feels like the right thing to do, so let's just go and do it."

KEY TAKEAWAYS

Each social enterprise profiled here took a unique path to finding a Purpose Point. The hard fact is that there is no single path to doing so, but the good news is that you can focus on the three fundamental commonalities pointed out throughout these stories in the ways that so many successful social innovators have honed in on the problems they've tackled and on what their product and business model would be.

1. Specify the Problem

The first step toward finding your Purpose Point is to identify a problem to tackle with enough specificity that you can differentiate your brand and tap into a market that can be effectively targeted. Narrowing down the distinctive contribution you want to make to fit your capabilities and to hone in on a community of early adopters is vital. Even behemoths like Coca-Cola and Nike must take carefully calibrated steps. Specificity is essential when identifying a social or environmental problem. By definition, social entrepreneurs are trying to solve some of the world's most challenging social and environmental problems such as poverty, oppression, inequity, climate change, and resource preservation. These problems are deep-rooted and complex, otherwise they would have been solved long ago. They can be sprawling and entirely overwhelming. Narrowing down your focus from a general problem to a specific, approachable one allows you to direct your energy in the more targeted fashion that will allow you to gain traction.

Key Question: How can I narrow my problem down? Are there ways I can make the problem more specific?

2. Leverage Cultural Shifts

Once you've identified a specific problem, you must step back to take a good hard look beyond the problem to the culture at large.

Shifts in culture, such as changes in the technology or in the increasing demand among consumers for better corporate behavior, can pose either a crisis or an opportunity for an organization. Failing to spot these trends may weaken established companies, while capitalizing on them can be powerful fuel in the making of a successful and impactful organization.

Key Question: What are the key cultural shifts relating to my problem? How can I leverage those shifts to my advantage?

3. Build on Talent

The last fundamental step in identifying your Purpose Point is to analyze how your unique mix of talents can be applied to solving the problem. In doing this you should:

- Consider your domain expertise, meaning your knowledge in a particular set of skills, such as design, marketing, computer programming, farming, or engineering.

- Next consider your sector expertise, meaning your understanding of the larger context of the problem you've honed in on, such as food, water, health care, or education.

- Finally, consider your personality and the type of work you generally gravitate toward. Ask yourself, are you an introvert or an extrovert? Do you most enjoy managing people or are you more of a tinkerer who enjoys building the mousetrap but doesn't like leading a team? Different types of problems will require different types of organization and different skills in creating and building the organization.

Honestly evaluating your talents and skill set in this way will allow you to identify the jobs you will be able to tackle yourself and those for which you should solicit the input or collaboration of others with expertise. No matter how much talent an entrepreneur possesses, he or she will never be talented enough to create a successful organization all alone. There's a strong myth in our culture of the lone innovative entrepreneur, but the truth is that no successful organization has been built by one sole person.

Building an effective social enterprise requires a multidisciplinary team that will provide competence in key areas and be able to challenge and refine thinking and decision making.

Key Question: What unique talents do I possess that will help solve my problem? Where are my weaknesses? How can I build a multidisciplinary team?

CHAPTER TWO

Design with Humility

After the social innovator has found her purpose point, the next phase is designing the product or service, moving from concept into action. Many founders feel a great sense of urgency to get up and running, and they are too hurried in launching and then give up too soon if the service or product doesn't take off right away. Another key problem in this phase is that once they've created a business plan, they follow the plan too rigidly, mistaking what should be only a rough guide for a fully worked-out business model. A third common mistake is believing that they have to have all the answers and should be able to design their product or service on their own or with only minimal input from others.

The myth of the brilliant founder who comes up with a groundbreaking new solution and then by ingenuity and sheer force of will builds a thriving organization all alone has done in many promising enterprises and stunted the growth of many others, leading them to hang on to flawed ideas too long and miss opportunities to improve their product and model.

As successful serial entrepreneur and leading expert on entrepreneurship Steve Blank wrote in his influential article "Why the Lean Start-Up Changes Everything," "Business plans rarely survive first contact with customers . . . Start-ups are not smaller versions of large companies. They do not unfold in accordance with master plans. The ones that ultimately succeed go quickly from failure to failure, all the while adapting, iterating on, and improving their initial ideas as they continually learn from customers."

Blank is one of the leaders of a fast-growing movement toward more user-focused and iterative product development, which includes both the approach recommended by Eric Ries, author of the influential book *The Lean Startup*, and the discipline of Human Centered Design.

Eric studied under Steve Blank at University of California, Berkeley, where he gained insight on the startup world. Eric also looked across the Pacific. What he found were lessons from the lean manufacturing methodology developed by Toyota, which he used to craft the lean startup method, described more fully here. That is, the lean method of manufacturing involves relentlessly removing all of the waste from the process and testing the product early and regularly as it is developed.

Ries combined these insights when crafting his Lean Startup Methodology. The basic methodology is: Build, Measure, Learn. In the Build phase, the designer should build the minimum viable product (MVP), which is a stripped-down version of the product that has only the features necessary to deploy the product and no more. It is intended to be quick and cheap to build and serve as a learning tool to understand what the users think about it. Next is the Measure phase, which is where the designer deploys the MVP and measures how users interact with the product. This is the stage to gain deep insights about the user and the product as the two interact. Finally, the Learn stage is when a designer takes the data from the design stage and gains clarity as to what is working and what is not. At this point it will likely be necessary to pivot, or make changes to the product, based on user feedback. Then the cycle begins again.

Human Centered Design (HCD) is design informed by empathy. For decades the famed design firm IDEO has been on the leading edge of innovation in design for some of the biggest companies in the world. In conjunction with the Bill & Melinda Gates Foundation and other partners, IDEO took their design process and revised it to solve problems in the developing world. The core of the process is empathy—a deep understanding of a user's life, even though the designer hasn't lived that life.

HCD is a process that starts with a specific design challenge and proceeds through three major steps: Hear, Create, Deliver. In the Hear step, designers collect stories and inspiration directly from the users through field research. In the Create phase, the designers gather in a workshop to take all of the research and identify themes and translate stories into a larger framework. Then, after identifying themes, the designers move back to concrete solutions and prototype. Finally, in the Deliver phase, the designers conduct rapid revenue and cost modeling and assess how the solution can be implemented.

The stories of successful social innovators clearly demonstrate the value of taking this user-focused and iterative approach to designing your product or service, and to working out your overall business model. Every one of the enterprises profiled in this book encountered unexpected setbacks and had to scramble to make improvements to their concepts or products, often making a substantial pivot away from the original plan. It's not important whether you follow the Lean Startup methodology or improvise your own particular development process, but what's vital is that you approach the process with a good dose of humility, not believing you've got answers, but rather that you're testing hypotheses, and that you move forward according to these three steps:

- Listen
- Build
- Iterate

In this chapter, we'll first spend some time with the innovative design firm D-Rev to learn about the methods they've developed for getting out in the field and listening to users, then building prototypes and testing them with users. We'll then see how Charles Best made great use of a minimal viable product to verify that he was onto a good idea and should go ahead and develop a more sophisticated web site. Then we'll go on the journey of discovery of the founders of Embrace as they worked to develop their baby warmer, to see how user feedback and pivoting were vital to their successful development of the product and entry into the difficult market in India.

BRINGING BRILLIANT DESIGN TO THE POOR

After more than two decades treating patients as a psychiatrist in Colorado, in 1981 Paul Polak decided to found an innovative social enterprise called International Development Enterprises, working to use the power of markets to remediate poverty by creating affordable irrigation technology and bringing water to millions of struggling farmers, allowing them to sustain a living. In 2007, he founded technology incubator Design Revolution, or D-Rev for short, with electrical engineer Kurt Kuhlman, to bring high quality, innovative design to the development of products for the poor. Top quality design had historically been available only to the top 10 percent of income earners. Very little top design manpower was focused on the world's extreme poor—those living on less than $2 a day. The concept of D-Rev is to use the marketplace as the indicator of how well they are designing products, selling the products to the extreme poor at very low cost, but not giving them away. If those with so little money will buy a product, that means it is truly serving their needs.

The founders managed to solicit the participation of world-class designers, and in order to take the organization to the next level, they brought in Krista Donaldson as CEO. Krista was a veteran in the discipline of design thinking; applying design principles to the development of better products and services. She had also been on the ground in East Africa as one of the first interns for a social enterprise called AproTec that designs and sells human-powered irrigation pumps to smallholder farmers. And she had spent a year and a half on the ground in Iraq, working on the design of the post-war electrical power grid.

In the early days of AproTec, they had focused on designing a great product for the smallholder farmers they wanted to sell to, but they had not developed a good distribution channel. Krista learned that you can design really great technology, but if you're not thinking about the path to the user, particularly with market-driven models, then you're not going to have an impact.

During her time in Iraq, the U.S. policy for reconstructing the power grid was largely focused on one thing, building power plants. They were not thinking strategically about the whole system and they weren't asking the right questions. For example, what kind of fuel is needed for a power plant? How is it going to be paid for? And what are the pricing structures? How will the system work at each link in the chain? The result was many delays and setbacks. Krista's takeaway from both experiences was that to solve such difficult problems, you've got to be thinking about all the moving parts in a system and how they impact each other.

On the day I caught up with Krista, the D-Rev lab was buzzing. The company was in talks with two different distribution groups for their anti-jaundice device for babies, called Brilliance. They had just found out that some countries wouldn't allow shipments from India, where they are manufacturing, so they were working on navigating the trade laws. At the same time they were about to start field trials for the Remotion Knee—an innovative prosthetic—in Indonesia. The design team had been staying late to wrap up all the regulatory compliance paperwork, which is pretty intense for medical devices. People were getting a little punchy from lack of sleep. They were also working on the protocols for the impact assessment required to launch the clinical trials for the knee, and there was a bottleneck in getting documentation translated from Indonesian to English. So people were frantically running around trying to get the last of the Indonesian protocol translated into English and printed.

Their mission is to develop products through innovative design to improve the health and incomes of people at the bottom of the pyramid. They design extremely low-cost products to be marketed and sold to the poorest people on the planet, but they hold themselves to world-class standards. This tension requires a great deal of innovation and inspiration throughout the design process. The lab is the heart of D-Rev but it's not the only location of product development. D-Rev engineers and designers spend much of their time in the far-flung regions of the world. Krista's experience in East Africa and Iraq taught her the lessons of integrating the entire business model—price points, distribution, maintenance, and the end users—into the design process.

With their baby products, D-Rev holds itself accountable to the standards of the American Academy of Pediatrics. Krista noted, "It's not just us saying, we're great. We are meeting these internationally recognized standards." This is critical because there are so many western organizations that claim to have the next silver bullet product for the bottom of the pyramid, but don't build to high quality standards. "I really believe that it doesn't matter what income level you are, you want a beautiful, high-functioning product," said Krista.

LETTING THE USERS GUIDE YOU

Krista demonstrates rigorous humility about the knowledge needed to come through on D-Rev's promise. "My personal perspective is that there are too many things in the social sector that are perceived problems and not real problems." In order to understand this, you need to spend a great deal of time on the ground talking to users, she says. Far too many aspiring entrepreneurs hatch their ideas and move right on to execution without taking time to ask the intended users what they think of the idea for the product or service.

At D-Rev, the user is at the center of every design decision. Krista explains, "Everything we've worked on at D-Rev since I've taken over has come from a doctor, a nurse, someone who has said we have this problem, we need help solving this." D-Rev is not in the business of identifying problems. They leave that to experts on the issues because they're on the ground day in and day out. D-Rev is in the business of listening to people who have more knowledge than them about problems.

Then they investigate themselves. They ask, is the problem widespread or isolated to a particular place or a few places? How are people solving the problem now? Have better solutions been crafted somewhere else? Then they try to understand if there is a business model that will allow them to solve the problem at a price point that will be economically viable.

The first step is to understand the needs of the user. D-Rev gathers a massive collection of requirements for every product. Not all of them are consistent with one another, and not all have equal weight; the designers carefully prioritize each of them.

For a new device in development, not yet launched and code-named Comet, they compiled a list of 40 different user requirements, such as: Is it easy to clean? and is it the best shape and size for shipping? After composing the full set, the team generates a spectrum of the requirements, a long process in which they evaluate the priority of each.

The next step is to create rough prototypes of various possible ways a product might develop. They then assess those rough versions and begin a long process of creating more polished prototypes through iteration. Failure is a vital part of the process. Krista says, "We follow Silicon Valley and encourage our designers to fail fast." They build and tweak to more fully align the product with the user requirements until they have a product they feel comfortable with for conducting user tests, where they monitor the usage of the product as well as ask questions about its functionality. Then they work with the user feedback to iterate some more. The process continues until they have satisfied their requirements and the test users are happy with the product—so happy that they will spend money to have it, even though they have so little.

User feedback always uncovers issues the designers haven't thought of and details about how the product is actually working or falling short. For instance, in testing a prosthetic knee one user told them "This is too bulky. That might be fine for you Westerners, but we have more delicate frames." That one comment revealed a serious design bias they hadn't recognized. On another occasion, the team was seeking feedback from a doctor in India on a medical device, and he told them, "You know you Westerners with your silver bullets. We just really want a comparable device that looks like what you have in Stanford Hospital, but it needs to work and we need to be able to afford it." The design community can focus on novelty too much, when it's really users' needs that matter, and users want something that solves their problem, whether it's a bold new solution or an established one.

In conducting tests and surveys, it's important to get feedback from a range of users because some of them may be reluctant to criticize the product, and some may be thinking of using it in a certain situation while others will be thinking of other situations. Users have biases, too.

D-Rev works hard on their surveys, asking the same questions in a number of different ways to try to eliminate any survey biasing and validate user responses. The team looks for a convergence in user feedback to guide them forward.

Users cannot, however, tell you everything you need to know about developing a product. They can give great feedback on the fit and feel of the prosthetic, for example, but can't tell you anything about its strength and durability with one or two try-ons. So D-Rev also does rigorous lab testing, such as conducting stress tests for the knee. Then they take all of the data from the lab and users and synthesize it to inform their design.

DISCOVERING YOU NEED TO PIVOT

One of the products D-Rev developed with this process is a phototherapy device called Brilliance that treats severely jaundiced babies. The device shines a blue light on a baby's skin, which breaks down a build up of a yellow pigment that can cause brain damage. The traditional devices used for treatment cost between $3,000 and $10,000, and Brilliance has the same or better effect at a cost of $400.

D-Rev identified the need for the device through research that showed that most mothers in the poor communities they are targeting give birth at home, and most of them have never heard of jaundice and don't know the symptoms to look for. This leads to delays in getting their babies to clinics, which is a terrible problem because jaundice must be treated early. Treatment was being further delayed because most rural clinics couldn't afford to buy the machines for treatment and babies had to be sent to hospitals in the nearby cities. So D-Rev set out to design a really affordable phototherapy device, which they intended to be sold to the rural clinics.

But as they conducted their fieldwork, visiting more than 300 clinics and hospitals, and in conducting a study in collaboration with researchers from Stanford University and other institutions, they discovered that almost 90 percent of public hospitals in the major urban areas also didn't have devices for the treatment. The team decided to pivot, focusing first on providing the machines to the larger hospitals because they were the centers of the highest demand for treatment, so they were where their machine could have the biggest impact.

DON'T UNDERESTIMATE THE CHALLENGES OF DISTRIBUTION

As Krista learned from her days in East Africa and Iraq, innovation in design must be applied not only to the development of the product but to the supply chain as well. In the case of the Brilliance machine, D-Rev targeted India as the first market to enter, and the nature of the Indian health care system posed a number of challenges. Krista knew that expertise would be required to negotiate the challenges, so D-Rev partnered with an Indian company called Phoenix, the largest producer of neonatal equipment in the country, to devise a novel distribution strategy.

The trick about the arrangement was that D-Rev wants the product to be sold primarily to rural hospitals and public hospitals in the city, not to private hospitals, which serve a relatively wealthy clientele. Phoenix, however, was incentivized to sell to the private hospitals because they could pay a higher price, resulting in a higher profit margin for Phoenix. So D-Rev structured a licensing agreement that instead incentivized selling the device to the rural and public hospitals over the private hospitals. Phoenix pays D-Rev a smaller licensing fee when they sell to rural or public hospitals than they do when they sell to private hospitals.

This is a great example of innovating by aligning profit and purpose. Rather than see the profit motive as a tension in their partnership, D-Rev chose to make good use of the profit motive. Brilliance launched successfully in India and has gone on to growing success in Africa as well, and the company is looking to bring it to Latin America and Southeast Asia.

YOU DON'T NEED TO BE AN EXPERT

D-Rev has developed a highly sophisticated methodology for product development, but you don't have to gain that kind of expertise to start implementing your plan. The scrappy way in which Charles Best went about testing his idea for Donors-Choose.org demonstrates that there's really no better way to start the process than simply by getting going.

Charles knew what he wanted to do for work from an early age. He was inspired by the impact his English teacher and his wrestling coach had on him to become a teacher. And since he loved history, he became a history teacher, taking a job in a public high school in a low-income community in the Bronx.

His colleagues would regularly discuss projects they wanted to do with their students but didn't have the supplies for, or a book they wanted to assign or a field trip they wished they could take their students on. The teachers were given very little discretion in the allocation of classroom resources, and money was extremely tight, with school budgets being cut year after year. Many teachers paid for supplies out of their own pockets, as is true all over the country.

Maybe it was the fact that Charles was still new to the system that made him think he could do something about this problem. He figured that there must be people out there who would want to help fund projects if they could see exactly where their money was going.

The little Charles knew about charity came from commercials and news coverage on TV and through direct mail solicitations, which were generally of the poverty porn variety. All the organizations seemed to want was people's money; they didn't seem interested in really getting people directly engaged in creating solutions. Charles thought that approach was wrong. He thought it would be better if donors could feel at least partial ownership of the process, and if they knew how their money was spent and got feedback from people they chose to help.

At this time, back in 2000, the Internet was just coming into its own and proving to be a powerful force in business. eBay had burst onto the scene and revolutionized the second-hand goods market, and that consumer-to-consumer model gave Charles an idea: Use the Internet to connect teachers who have great ideas for projects and can't afford the materials they need with donors who get to choose which project they want to support.

Charles didn't conduct any analysis or write a detailed strategic plan in pursuing the idea. He recalls, "I didn't know enough to even do a survey of the Web and what was out there. Because I didn't have ambition for this to be a national organization." He simply saw a problem his colleagues were facing and he thought he had a good idea for solving it, and he just decided to go ahead and give it a shot.

Back then, nobody had really tapped the power of the Internet for fundraising, so there were no real models for that to follow. The closest model seemed to be the commercial one of eBay, and from the outset many people were calling DonorsChoose.org a philanthropic eBay (though, now it is, much more appropriately referred to as a Kickstarter for public school classrooms).

Charles knew nothing about building a website; he had no knowledge or programming experience. He did, however, have experience in woodworking and he saw the two skills as related. As he says, "Woodworking is in some ways similar to web development in that at the planning stage you have to think through every scenario, and how each element is going to plug in to another element. You have to map it out and plan it perfectly. But no matter how carefully you've planned, stuff is going to come up, and it's not going to fit together perfectly. So you have to adjust and improvise." Charles loved this process, and he dove into planning his web site eagerly.

He just used paper and pencil to draft the wireframes for the pages—these are the drawings that programmers work from to code a site. Then he hired a programmer, recently arrived from Poland, who he found through a directory search. He was willing to do all of the programming for the site for $2,000.

This first iteration was a very simple site. All that was really needed to see if his idea would work was a listing of classroom project requests for people to browse through, and the site consisted essentially of one long page. The back end was even simpler. As Charles recalls, "You'd have to scroll down that page for like 15 minutes to get to the teacher or the project record that you were looking for." The page also included the boxes for users to enter their credit card numbers and passwords into, totally unencrypted. A donor would type in an amount that she wanted to donate, and enter her credit card number, but the site didn't actually do the processing of the credit card information; Charles reentered it by hand into the kind of countertop credit card terminal used by many small businesses. Typically, two weeks after the donor had donated, the transaction would finally be processed. This is a great case of a minimum viable product. It wasn't pretty, but it allowed Charles to test his idea with real donors.

To encourage his colleagues to post projects on the site he lured them with his mother's famous roasted pear dessert, which he set out on a table in the teacher's lounge. If someone wanted a pear, he'd say "Hold up. There is a toll. If you eat one of those you have to go to this new web site called DonorsChoose.org, and ask for whatever it is you most want for your students. Propose the project that you've always wanted to do with them." His colleagues were more than happy to post projects, but some admitted they didn't have high expectations that the site would actually raise any money. Sure enough, after the first set of 11 projects were posted, he waited for the magic to happen but got a resounding non-response.

Charles hadn't really thought about how to get word out, and he'd only told some friends and family members. His aunt funded one of the projects, but that was it. So he decided that he would fund the remaining 10 projects himself, anonymously. Since he was living rent free with his parents, he could spare a bit of his teacher's salary. That was the trigger; as soon as his colleagues saw that the other projects had been funded, word ripped through the Bronx schools and teachers started posting hundreds of projects.

Charles still had lots of work to do to actually build a better site, create a viable business model, and bring in donors, but with such a simple experiment he was able to generate strong evidence that teachers would come onboard. He was confident that even if it took a little time, donors would too. As we'll see in the next chapter, plenty of hustle was required to get DonorsChoose.org to really take flight, but Charles got the extra edge of enthusiasm and commitment he needed to see that process through from this very inexpensive and quick product launch.

Charles's original idea for his organization turned out to be fundamentally sound and the model stayed essentially the same as he perfected it. Such was not the case with the long and complex process of launching the Embrace Warmer, the innovative, low-cost incubator. Jane Chen and her team had to make many pivots over the course of several years of development and rollout.

EMBRACING CHALLENGES

Jane Chen and her team at Stanford working on developing their low-cost incubator had a clear idea of what they thought were the requirements for their product. They needed to create an incubator that would work without electricity, and was mobile and simple enough for a new mother or a midwife to use. But even with such a clear concept, actually making such a device turned out to be a challenge full of pivots.

The first step was coming up with a basic design, and they thought through many possibilities, including a tent-style device. Then, with the deadline for the project fast approaching, they did what any good students would do; they put on a pot of coffee, stocked up on Red Bull, and pulled an all-nighter. Finally, as the sun was starting to rise, they landed on an idea they thought had real promise. The design would resemble a tiny sleeping bag. The core heating technology would be a phase-change material, a wax-like material contained in plastic packets that when heated in boiling water maintains a constant temperature for eight hours. The packets could be slipped into a pocket in the back of the sleeping bag, and they could be reheated over and over again. They decided to call the device the Embrace Warmer.

This solution met all of their design criteria; it required no electricity, it was easily portable, intuitive to use, and it could be produced at a very low price point. As a bonus, the design would also work well in a variety of cultures, as mothers all around the globe warm their babies by wrapping them in blankets and holding them close to their own warm bodies. Finally, the sleeping bag could be easily sanitized by boiling it, making it easy to ensure a bacteria-free environment, crucial for a vulnerable newborn.

By the time the semester ended, they had tweaked the design enough that they knew they had something that might be able to work. Others agreed. They won both the Echoing Green fellowship, given to a select few social entrepreneurs every year, as well as a Stanford business plan competition. The team incorporated as a nonprofit, calling the organization Embrace.

Even armed with their Stanford degrees and such expert support, they had a great deal to learn, and the humility they brought to the process allowed them to listen effectively and to make many alterations to their plan.

Knowing that it would be foolish to try to launch the warmer globally, they decided to focus on one market, and after doing some research, they found that one out of every three babies in India are born with low birth weight and that more than one million die every year. So, they chose India.

A number of trips to India revealed to them that in order to truly understand the customers, the manufacturing issues, and the ins and outs of the distribution system, they would need to move to India. A side advantage of the move was that it kept costs low at this critical early product development stage. They could be with their customers and keep overhead low: win-win.

Once on the ground in India, they began meeting with anybody and everybody who could give them advice and feedback. In the first year they spoke with more than 150 stakeholders, from doctors, to mothers, to manufacturers, to hospital administrators.

One of their early discoveries was that boiling water wouldn't be an adequate heat source for the Embrace. Most of the Indian healthcare system is comprised not of large modern hospitals, but of one-room primary health clinics staffed by one doctor serving a whole village or rural region. More often than not, when a baby is born with low birth weight in these primary care health clinics, the doctor recommends a transfer to a hospital in the nearest town, and that journey is often long and dangerous due to road conditions. For these journeys, boiled water would not be viable.

So they decided they would produce two versions, one for the home, which would be heated by boiled water, and one for clinics and hospitals, which would be heated by electricity. Again their decision had an unexpected benefit. The electricity-powered model resolved safety concerns among doctors and clinicians about the use of boiled water, which smoothed the way to gaining their support. An added side-effect of this was the credibility the doctors' approval earned them among the public, which has great respect for the doctors and the professional healthcare system. Yet another benefit of splitting the product line was that they could charge a higher price for the clinical model, earning extra profit with which to fund the continual product development of the home version. For all of these reasons, they decided to bring the clinical model to market first.

Simply by spending quality time on the ground and asking stakeholders about the product they wanted, the team was able to greatly improve their model.

USER TESTING HAS MANY BENEFITS

Designing a breakthrough product is fairly meaningless if it can't be manufactured and distributed for the right price point, and the Embrace team still had lots of work to do to make the products viable. For one thing, they were up against the considerable skepticism any truly new product tends to face, let alone one you are asking doctors and mothers to use with vulnerable babies. They knew they needed high-quality product testing. First they tested with mannequins, then they moved to testing with full-term healthy babies and finally, they moved to a small randomized, controlled trial on low birth-weight babies who were experiencing cold stress.

The results of all the testing were positive. The product kept babies at a constant temperature, and it was able to bring babies with cold stress back to a healthy body temperature. In fact, the Embrace Warmer actually outperformed the current standards of care in the hospitals. They seemed to have exceeded their goal. But plenty of discoveries lay ahead of them, requiring yet more pivots.

KNOWING WHAT TO OUTSOURCE

Like any startup, Embrace had limited resources and people, so they wanted to run lean—focusing on what they are good at and outsourcing the rest. Their core competencies were design and strategy, so they decided to outsource manufacturing and sales.

As they pursued their plan for manufacturing, they learned one of the fundamental lessons anyone who produces a new product confronts: manufacturing is a challenging process. For the uninitiated, it seems so simple; you just give the specs to a manufacturer and a perfectly made widget appears. If only that were the case. There are so many steps in the process that many different kinds of mistakes can be made, and manufacturing a brand new product is especially prone to errors. The Embrace team was also working with a language barrier, and it somehow had to get high-grade, clinical-quality production at an extremely low cost.

Jane quickly realized that simply outsourcing the process wouldn't work. She recalls, "You have to micromanage the hell out of the process to make sure that you are getting the quality that you need. What we ultimately ended up finding was that for some components, it was better to do it in-house." Embrace brought the making of the more complicated components in-house, such as the wax pouch, and though the work was difficult, they managed to come up with a way of producing the pouches that are higher quality than those of the original manufacturer, and they produce them for less cost. Embrace also takes charge of the final assembly and the quality control.

The unexpected side benefit of this pivot was that Embrace has developed valuable expertise in manufacturing. Thus, should they ever outsource some components of manufacturing in the future, the in-house team will know exactly how to direct the process.

FINDING EARLY ADOPTERS TAKES WORK

The Embrace team also had to learn to be very strategic about whom they targeted for their first sales. The Indian healthcare system is bifurcated, comprised of both pubic and private hospitals, and Embrace wanted to be in both. But the sales cycle in a public hospital is much longer due to the relationships that need to be built and the bureaucracy to be navigated. So, in order to get to market in a timely manner, they decided to focus first on private hospitals. The team's solid understanding of the Indian healthcare landscape shaped the Embrace go-to-market strategy to optimize for efficient use of time and money as well as the greatest chance for early wins. Again, they were willing to make a significant pivot. Their whole project had begun with the intent to get the warmers to poor women in villages, but they recognized that instead they should target the parts of the market that they could make the most headway with the most readily.

They still needed a strategy for actually getting the warmers into the hands of the doctors, and the team decided to test numerous strategies simultaneously. One was to sell through the pharmaceutical reps already visiting the doctors on a regular basis. Another was to work with a nonprofit that focused on sales and distribution of medical devices. The nonprofit would create a dedicated sales force for the warmer, funded by Embrace. The third strategy was to work through the stores called stockists in India, which are the wholesalers for medical products. Finally, they would partner with GE Healthcare, which made an agreement with Embrace for a minimum purchase. In the deal, GE obtained global sales and distribution rights but would begin in India. This deal carried two great bonuses; it lent the credibility of working with a huge well-respected partner, and the guaranteed minimum order allowed Embrace to make some basic revenue projections.

They launched the product in the summer of 2011, and as well planned as their strategy was, the next year was still one of learning how incremental the process of building awareness and breaking into a market can be.

CREATING DEMAND

Need for a product and demand for it are two different things. There was a clear need for the Embrace Warmer, but demand had to be created. This is particularly the case when you are bringing a new product to market that requires a behavior change. Generally, in order to move from need to demand, a company has to invest a significant amount of effort and resources in educating the potential consumers. Putting distribution in the hands of outside parties, as Embrace had, makes this more difficult. Embrace was to learn another valuable lesson here about outsourcing. The warmer simply wasn't being pushed vigorously by any of their distributors. Even the GE deal wasn't leading to the growth in sales Embrace needed. All of the distributors they chose had other products they were selling, all of which had a much higher profit margin, so the warmer just wasn't a priority.

The team realized that, as Jane says, "You can't have the same sales force selling the higher end and the lower end products. You need to separate sales forces." So they decided to pivot yet again and build out their own sales force. At first they hired sales people fresh out of college, known as *Freshers* in India. This is a common practice in the country, and it seemed like a good idea; they'd be low cost and, since they are fresh out of school, very trainable. Freshers have proven a great success in many sectors. But it turned out that whereas, Freshers work well for pharmaceutical sales, because the doctors they are selling to already know about the drugs, for a new product a more sophisticated sales force is required. The salesperson must have the ability to persuasively educate the doctor about the product. This requires skill, confidence, experience, and maturity. So, Jane knew that they needed to pivot yet again. They hired a team of experienced salespeople who would focus on key influencers in specifically targeted hospitals. They began to get some traction.

GOOD NEWS TRAVELS SLOW

The early response from the medical community was very positive, which was helped by another smart decision the team made. They wanted to ensure that the first products on the market were being used properly, so they scheduled multiple follow-up visits with the doctors and nurses using the device, and in this process they collected a whole book of testimonials to use in sales.

Then they got a lucky break that accelerated adoption. As the saying goes, "Sometimes it's better to be lucky than good." But it's best if you can be both lucky and good. The Embrace team was introduced to the Health Secretary of the state of Rajasthan, and it turned out that his daughter had recently had a premature baby. He had direct experience with the problem, and he understood the concept of the warmer and the need for it immediately. He decided to test the device in every hospital in one of his districts. The nurses reported they found the warmer incredibly easy to use.

This led Embrace to propose a series of smaller pilots with public hospitals in other areas They hired a case study coordinator to collect data from these programs. The results showed that 77 percent of premature babies were hypothermic and confirmed that after placing those babies in the Embrace device they were able to maintain a normal body temperature.

As a result of the positive data coming out of both the private hospitals and the public pilot programs in the public hospitals, Embrace started to gain traction among the broader public healthcare system in India. Twenty months after launch in the private hospital system, the company got its first big entry into the public hospital system. The state of Karnataka issued a directive to 258 government hospitals, providing them funding to purchase the device. By the end of 2013, Embrace was in every hospital in the state.

Now Embrace is seeing a domino effect, with additional state adoptions.

While D-Rev has developed a rigorous methodology for learning from end users and then iterating a product until it will sell to them, Embrace learned the same lessons about the value of on-the-ground learning and making pivots in your development process by simply forging ahead with open minds and a great deal of persistence. The humility displayed by Jane Chen and her team, by Charles Best in launching his simple site, and even by the experienced pros at D-Rev in facing the many frustrating challenges the developing world throws at any social innovator makes all the difference. Those who want to successfully enter these complicated markets must not only get to know their end users and all of those at the vital links in the food chain from production through to distribution, they must genuinely want to learn from them.

KEY TAKEAWAYS

1. Listen

Good design starts not with doing, but with listening. Listening assumes that the user knows better than the designer. The designer should be interacting with the target users in their environment to gain both qualitative and quantitative insights about what kind of product or service they really need and want, how those needs and wants are prioritized, and how the context impacts those needs and wants.

The goal in the listening phase is to get as close as possible to a holistic understanding of the end user's pain points and desires. This cannot be done in the office or in a lab. This requires not only the research out in the field, but aggregating all of the data so that you move from a set of individual stories to higher-level insights. You must make sense of the data by identifying patterns.

Key Question: What do the users want?

2. Build

After collecting, aggregating, and weighting the insights gained from the intended users and developing clear specifications, you are ready to roll up your sleeves and start building.

You should test your assumptions early on with a minimum viable product that you share with actual targeted end users. It's important that your product is well-enough conceived and constructed that it isn't rejected simply because of the execution of your design and gives users a good taste of how they might benefit from the product. This way, they are more motivated to engage with your questions about the product and to help you make improvements.

Key Question: How can I quickly and cheaply build an MVP to get my product in the hands of users as quickly as possible?

3. Iterate

You should go into the testing process with the assumption that your product will fail in some way, and that it might even turn out to be the wrong product entirely. You must not only be willing to pivot, you've got to be constantly keeping your eye out for signs that a pivot is required. Becoming comfortable with the idea that you will fail, perhaps many times, before you succeed will be invaluable in persevering through all the variables.

There are multiple methodologies for assessing the responses to your MVP. After receiving user feedback you must sort through all the data in order to find actionable metrics. This often involves serious grappling with the question of whether to pivot away from your plan or to forge ahead, or perhaps make just very moderate changes. You should go into the process expecting to go through several cycles of iteration.

Key Question: How can user feedback improve the MVP?

This process shouldn't end even after you've launched your product. You want to be continuously listening, building, and iterating in order to find more ways to serve your users.

CHAPTER THREE

Build with Hustle

"If you want to build a ship, don't drum up people together to collect wood and don't assign them tasks and work, but rather teach them to long for the endless immensity of the sea."

—Antione de Saint-Exupéry

Newton's first law of motion dictates that an object stays at rest until acted upon by force. Even if that object is the best-designed product, it will never be successfully launched without exerting the right amount of force to get it in motion. That is what the building phase is all about—igniting the momentum necessary to launch a great product and a great company.

The most important factor in this phase is *hustle*.

So many pieces need to fall in place, from press to design to distribution, and at the prelaunch stage getting support and funding can take a good deal of persuasion. This is a messy process for many founders, of fits and starts, with daily challenges and many setbacks. Just think of how many of those the Embrace team had to overcome. Often the only way to succeed is with a great amount of audacity, energy, passion, and sheer hustle to rally all of the resources, people, and financing required.

Many great products never progress beyond this stage because the social innovator was not able to build the necessary momentum. There are many lessons about how to persevere and tactics for generating momentum from founders who have been willing to work every connection and try every angle.

THE INTUITIVE HUSTLE

When Scott Harrison developed his concept for Charity: Water he thought he could solve the water problem in five years, then he'd move on to the next issue, perhaps Charity: Education or Charity: Health. His ambition was huge; he didn't just set out to solve specific problems, he thought the whole charity system was broken and he wanted to fix it.

He had identified three major problems. First, the non-profit world was generally horrible at storytelling. Second, the branding was mediocre at best. Third, there was little transparency about operations and results.

Scott's friends saw charity as simply a black hole—you threw money into it and nothing came out of it. His generation was particularly disaffected. They had grown up watching the famines in Ethiopia on TV and listening to songs like "We Are The World." Millions were raised. But nobody knew where the money was going. Then a number of stories broke about the misuse of funds by a few poorly run charities. Scott believed that for Charity: Water to be successful, he had to change how reporting was done about use of funds.

He decided that all of the money he raised for water projects, 100 percent of it, would go directly to the projects. None would go to the overhead for running the organization, and Charity: Water would be completely open with its finances. He wanted people to see where their money was going, so Charity: Water would photograph all of the projects and install GPS monitors on them, so that they would be easy to find on Google Earth. To keep the funds for the water projects completely separate from funds he would have to raise specifically for overhead, he would set up two bank accounts.

Then there was the organization's look and messaging. He had learned the power of strong branding from club promotion. If you spent just a little more money and hired a graphic designer, you could have more beautiful invitations that would bring the right crowd to an event. He would apply that lesson to Charity: Water. At that time, most charity web sites looked like sites for insurance companies, and Scott knew there was no reason Charity: Water's branding shouldn't be as stunning as that for a high-end fashion brand. He worked with his friends in graphic design to build an iconic brand.

His final secret weapon would be powerful photography to tell the organization's story. He'd been able to tell a compelling story for Mercy Ships through his photography. Even his friends that he knew were easily bored had been powerfully moved. He compiled a set of photos and loaded them onto his laptop.

So he had a basic game plan. His ambition was bold, but he was still living on people's couches when he came up with these ideas. He knew that if he was going to gain support, he was going to have to really hustle.

He started running all over the city giving seven to twelve presentations per day, sitting down with people, pulling out his laptop, and flipping through pictures to tell the story of the issue and of his vision for the organization. Fortunately, Scott is a gifted storyteller, but even so, it took a good deal of cajoling to get any momentum going. A first success was that one brave soul, a friend of his from his Mercy Ships-days named Laney, who decided she wanted to help out. She believed in the vision so much that she flew to New York and started working with Scott for no pay, also crashing on friends' couches.

The web site was up and running and Scott decided to throw a big launch party to raise money, again drawing on his club promotion expertise and using his connections to get a club to give him the space for free. He scheduled the party for the day of his thirtieth birthday, September 7, 2006. The party netted $15,000, and the organization was able to dig its first well.

The next month, he and Laney staged an ambitious outdoor exhibition in Central Park. The exhibition featured photos of dirty water sources in Africa and invited the crowd to experience what it was like to lack access to clean water.

Scott recalls, "I got a friend to build these crazy tanks, and we hustled the printers to give us a great deal on printing the photographs. I found out who I needed to make friends with in the parks department. Penske donated a truck, and we convinced hundreds of volunteers to help out." In just its first two months, Charity: Water had created a splash among a set of key influencers in New York.

A few more young and passionate people came on board then. Vik, a talented graphic designer took a pay cut and gave up her health insurance to join, and Becky Straw, fresh out of graduate school at Columbia, came on to direct the water programs. An ever-growing army of volunteers supplemented the team, and they began to run operations out of Scott's Soho loft apartment. They would work from early morning until 11:00 at night, sleep for a few hours, and do it again. Scott continued running all over the city for meetings. The volunteers cold called organizations to request donations of whatever they needed—printing, transportation, supplies for promotions. An organization couldn't be more scrappy. People found the work exhilarating and Scott worked relentlessly. One day when a group of volunteers was painting the walls of the apartment and had covered the floor with a drop cloth, Scott couldn't stop his work just to get the office painted. So he just lifted up the cloth and sat under it working on his laptop while the painting continued.

He was not ashamed to go back to people again and again to try to get them onboard. At one point, he was trying to get the magazine *Marie Claire* to write a piece, but they kept putting him off, so he just showed up at the lobby, called the editor and said "I'm downstairs in your lobby. Let's talk." So, they finally gave him an interview and ran a piece on his fledgling organization. He would recruit anybody to help, people he encountered on an elevator, the servers at restaurants, anyone he could get to listen to him.

His first meetings came about just through random recommendations. A New York socialite who followed Scott's emails hooked him up to meet with a friend at Swarovski. That friend connected him to the VP of Saks Fifth Avenue, which ultimately led to Saks supporting a global campaign. It was an inefficient and nonlinear approach, but it's what was necessary to get the money to slowly trickle in.

A key fundraising technique was selling the $20 bottles of water displaying the Charity: Water logo. The bottles looked elegant. The branding wasn't depressing. The message was direct and empowering: buying this bottle will help one person get access to ongoing clean water. The bottles sold well, and because the group had no office yet, volunteers were recruited to do the labeling. True to the mission, 100 percent of the cash went straight into digging wells.

A year later, after learning more about the environmental hazards of bottled water, the team realized they didn't really need to sell the bottles. The concept of an average donor giving a tiny amount of money to provide clean drinking water for one person on the other side of the globe was powerful enough on its own, and they moved into digital promotions, starting with email campaigns and sending e-cards. Every holiday was an excuse to launch a campaign: Valentines Day, Mother's Day, Father's Day. They found ways to craft a message for each occasion, and these campaigns were effective. The donor base grew and the flow of money increased from a trickle to a small stream, with all of the money still going to digging wells.

Scott was committed to putting 100 percent of the funds raised from the public toward water projects. But, obviously, they needed to pay for the operations of the organization, so they raised money separately for operations. They had also convinced a handful of donors to give money to a second account, toward operations to pay salaries and keep, and maybe get an office. Scott recalls, "To fund operations, we were just scraping $10,000 here, $15,000 here, from board members and friends." But that wasn't enough. About a year and a half after the launch, they hit a huge snag: they were almost broke. Though they were raising a good deal of money to fund the water projects, they couldn't convince enough people to give to their operations.

The problem with the 100-percent-to-projects model, especially at the beginning when an organization hasn't proven success yet, is that nobody wants to fund operations.

According to Scott, "It's almost impossible. This is why I don't preach the 100 percent model."

When an organization commits to the 100 percent model, it's really committing to fundraise with two very distinct groups of donors. The group that gives to programs is that of the mass-market donors who will make generally small contributions. The second group, which gives to operations, is comprised of large donors cutting checks in the tens and hundreds of thousands of dollars.

Scott hadn't focused enough on this second group. As he recalls, "I hadn't been able to get people to care about paying for staff and operations. I was probably too focused on water projects."

The result was that 18 months after launching, they had only five weeks of money left in the operational fund. Unless some miracle happened, it appeared they weren't going to be able to continue with the 100 percent model. Many trusted advisors suggested Scott borrow money from the water account to use for operations. Their argument was that as the organization's reputation grew, Scott could bring in many more operational donors and the money could be paid back to the account for the wells. But Scott felt that if he dipped into the water fund even once and in a temporary way, that would be the start of heading down a slippery slope, and they would become like every other charity. More importantly, he had made a promise to his donors. His integrity was at stake.

He decided he would rather fail with a model he was committed to than succeed by compromising on it. He would keep hustling as hard as he could to raise operational funding, but he was prepared to fail. He recalls, "I was going to shut down and grant out the remaining money for wells. I thought we'd just have to do a reboot, and start over without the 100 percent model."

Then, something happened that saved them from the brink. Call it a lucky break or an answered prayer, but it saved Charity: Water from failing. These breaks seem to be a matter of sheer luck, but in fact they're the result of all of the passion and relentless push that lead up to them.

One day, very shortly before the operational funds would run out, Scott made a pitch to entrepreneur Michael Birch, who had just sold his company, Bebo, to AOL for $850 million. They sat down for two hours and Scott gave it all he had, but he didn't think the meeting went particularly well. Birch hadn't seemed interested.

At midnight that day, Scott was sitting in his bed checking his emails, stressing about how he was save the organization, when he received an email from Michael saying he just wired $1 million into the operations account. Charity: Water would survive. The $1 million donation gave the team 13 months of runway to hone their model and find more larger-scale funders.

THE STRATEGIC HUSTLE

Scott Harrison and his team grew Charity: Water in a classic bootstrapping, by-the-seat-of-the pants style, with no real business plan. The founders of Warby Parker took a very different approach, conducting extensive market research, even taking a class at Wharton on the market issues they would face, and creating a detailed business plan early. Though, as you'll see, their approaches were vastly different, they both required an immense amount of hustle.

A month after they committed to work on the business, they all enrolled in a class called Healthcare Entrepreneurship. The only deliverable in the class was a business plan.

During the course, they conducted in-depth industry analysis, and what they discovered was astounding. One company, Luxottica, pretty much has a monopoly on the entire eyewear industry. It owns Oakley, Ray-Ban, Oliver Peoples, Persol, and Arnette among others. It also licenses the Ralph Lauren and Chanel names, as well as those of pretty much every other fashion label you have heard of. The company is also vertically integrated, owning Sunglass Hut, Lens Crafters, Pearl Vision, Sears Optical, and Target Optical. The icing on the cake is that it owns the second largest vision insurance plan. So it makes money manufacturing, licensing, and selling glasses as well as providing insurance for the consumer to support purchases. It does quite well, with more than $2 billion in revenue in 2013.

Luxottica was able to take the Ray Ban brand, which was selling in gas stations for $30 in the 1970s, to a $200 purchase now. Even accounting for inflation, that's quite a feat. This was the answer to the question of why a product that's essentially made with a 500-year-old technology costs $300 to $400, even more than an iPhone. A company with this much market power could easily crush a small startup.

On the other hand, this research convinced them they'd spotted a huge opportunity to compete on price. Luxottica wouldn't want to come down to their pricing—that would upend the Luxottica business model. The industry really was ripe for disruption.

Their initial plan was to sell their glasses for $45. But when they asked a pricing expert at Wharton, Professor Ronju Johori, he immediately shot that down. He taught them a vital lesson all founders must heed, explaining that no matter how good your cost analysis is, your cost of goods will always increase as you get to the actual manufacturing, and then keep increasing over time, which will leave you with increasingly slimmer margins, making it more difficult to fend off competitors. So you must build in some margin.

He also explained that even if they could bring the price down that low and still make money, a price point of $45 for quality glasses was outside the realm of believability for the consumer. He said that by pricing so low, they would cause consumers to think they were running a scam. Pricing too low erodes consumers' trust in the quality of a brand.

The meeting was transformative, and they decided to do a survey to nail the price, which they sent out to about 1,000 friends and classmates. Actually, they sent out five or six versions, tweaking the pricing to discover how high they could go before people said they wouldn't pay. The surveys were conducted electronically, including a mock up of the homepage with an image of a pair of glasses along with a price, and they asked just one question: "How willing are you to buy this pair of glasses on a scale of zero to ten?" They found that willingness to purchase increased with price up to about $100, then first plateaued and then dropped. So they knew they would charge just a little less than $100, but they had painstaking debates on whether that should be $95 versus $99 or $96 or $98 or $90. Finally they decided that $95 looked deliberate and was aesthetically appealing.

The team also researched the business models of startups they admired, such as Zappos, to learn about the ins and outs of customer service, and they leaned heavily on lessons about design from Apple. Anyone who walks into the beautiful Warby Parker store in Soho in Manhattan, across the street from the Apple store, will clearly see what they learned from Apple about store design. They also met with almost every professor in the marketing department to get advice, such as that from Professor David Bell who told them that word of mouth is the most effective promotional tool because the lifetime value of customers who come in through word of mouth channels versus paid advertising channels is higher.

In short, they had done a great deal of research and had created a very strong model before they launched. But they still took the bootstrapping approach, relying on their own investments of $25,000 each—splitting equity in the company equally—for their startup funding rather than seeking outside funds. They also continued with graduate school while they worked toward launch, and three of the four worked at internships during the summer before launch, hedging their bets about whether the company would take off by continuing to build strong resumes. And even their detailed planning didn't prevent them from facing a crisis they had to hustle their way out of once they launched.

The founders decided not to take on any staff and instead divided the labor among themselves. They also decided against renting any space; Neil's apartment would act as the head office, warehouse, and fulfillment center. They divided the work between the four. Andy and Neil focused on developing the product and marketing while Jeff and Dave focused on operations, all the while still taking highly demanding business classes. Andy and Neil spent a lot of time on the design of the collection as well as branding and PR, traveling to New York to meet with editors in the press as well as writing copy and drawing the wireframes for the web site. Meanwhile, Dave and Jeff spent their time working on fulfillment and with the programmers building out the back end of the web site to handle customer relations and finances.

BEST LAID PLANS

From the beginning the team had decided that they would spend their limited resources solely on three things: designing and manufacturing the collection, building the web site, and public relations to build brand credibility.

There are many strategies to bring customer awareness to a new brand. They could have taken out ads in magazines, advertised on social media, or created a search engine marketing strategy, but given their limited amount of cash, they decided to go with getting press coverage. Neil explains, "We thought that was going to be much more effective and much cheaper than paid acquisition." They had also been told about the superior value of word of mouth, and press would be the best generator of that; no matter how clever, ads just don't generate that kind of buzz. They had a cause, not just a product, and they believed they could get the press onboard.

Neil knew a little bit about PR because his wife had launched a successful jewelry company and before that had worked in PR at Yves St. Laurent. But this was a job for which they decided to go to a professional. Being deliberate business school students and former marketing consultants, they took this process very seriously, interviewing 40 different PR firms. Forty!

In the end, they decided to work with Patrick Bradbury from Bradbury Lewis, whose personal style they liked and who seemed to have built authentic relationships with editors and stylists as opposed to the approach of so many PR people of just calling and harassing editors constantly. Patrick delivered and was able to get them meetings with editors from *GQ* and *Vogue*. They went into high-gear hustle mode and not only sold the editors on the brand, but convinced them to feature the company's launch in their March issues. Getting coverage in the biggest women's and men's fashion magazines, in the same month no less, was no small feat for a startup brand.

Meanwhile the team still had a ton of work to do before launch. One big issue was that, as is always the case, the web site was taking longer to build than scheduled. (Seriously, in all my years, I've never seen or heard of a web site launching on time.) Then suddenly, they got a call from *GQ* saying that the magazine was going to be on stands the next day and asking why their site wasn't up. They hadn't gotten the information about when the issues would land. Neil recalls, "We called our developer and said listen, I don't care what state it is in, just get it up." They didn't tell any of their friends or family that the site was going live because they didn't know if it was actually going to work and they didn't want to be embarrassed if it didn't. It was launched just in time, and the developer was still finding bugs and trying to fix them.

On February 25, the March issue of *GQ* landed and orders immediately started to trickle in. Friends and family members started calling to say "Hey, your web site is live, do you know that?" The site was working, but over the weekend the trickle of orders turned into a deluge. Mayhem ensued.

A key part of Warby Parker's model was that they allowed customers to try on five frames at home—the home try-on program. The up side of the home try-on program was that customers could make more informed decisions, the downside is that they had to have five pairs on hand for every pair they sell. The initial launch far exceeded their projections. They were stunned by the response, and they fell victim to one of the most difficult problems the makers of new products face: inventory control. They realized that they were going to blow through their inventory and wouldn't be able to fulfill all the orders.

The team was at Neil's apartment, and they sat around the kitchen table debating about what to do, torn between letting the orders continue to come or suspending the home try-on program until they could ramp up inventory, which would take several months. The tension was brutal; Dave had set his cell phone to notify him every time an order was placed, and it just kept pinging. He said to them, "Guys over the last five minutes while we've been discussing this we've received 10 more orders." And the pace of orders just continued to increase. They had to make a decision fast.

One of their core values was to treat others the way you want to be treated, and they came to the conclusion that they would rather not make a promise they knew they could not fulfill. They thought if they were the customers, they'd rather be dealt with honestly.

They considered continuing to take orders but telling customers that they wouldn't be fulfilled for several months, but in the end they decided they didn't want customers to feel tricked in any way. If they were looking only for a short-term, transactional relationship with customers, maybe they would have gone that route, and it would have paid off in lots of immediate cash. Who knows how many more orders would have come in over the next months. But they were looking to build long-term relationships with customers. Neil explains, "We want to build a 100-year company. We want to build relationships with customers for their entire life. You only do that if you treat them with respect and trust and are transparent with them."

So, they made a hard decision; only a few days after their site they went live, Warby Parker decided to suspend the home try-on program. They explained the situation to their customers on the site, telling them they were humbled by the overwhelming response and were all out of frames, and asking for their email addresses so they could send a notice when they were back in stock. It was a good call. Once they were restocked, business picked right up again.

They still boot-strapped operations for a while, taking care of customer service themselves. They used Google voice to transfer calls to their cell phones. When a customer called, all of their cell phones would ring, and whoever answered first would deal with the call. They'd be sitting around Neil's apartment and everybody's cell phones would be buzzing, at all hours. They ended up skipping classes to handle the calls, and staying up late to answer customer emails. Sales continued to increase, and they hit their sales goals for the first year in just a few weeks.

Meanwhile they were in legitimate danger of flunking out of school, so they decided to make their first hire, bringing on one of their classmate's wives, Mara Castro, to handle customer service part time. They advertised the job as a 20-hour per week position, but in the first week she worked 90 hours. A year later, she would be leading a team of 80.

By a small miracle, the guys all ended up graduating. They had hustled their way through two years that were insanely busy and, before long, they were able to build a staff and move into an actual office, on 16th Street and Union Square in Manhattan.

BEATING THE BURN RATE

The founders of Method had decided to take on the consumer goods behemoths not only before they had a product, but even before they had a name. They had agreed that it would somehow refer to cleaning being about the technique, not about brute force, but after quite a bit of time batting ideas around, they were still stumped. Then suddenly, while Eric was brushing his teeth, he yelled out "Method," toothbrush still in his mouth.

Adam loved it, and it stuck.

So they had a concept and they had a name, but still no product. Their phenomenal success may make the fate of the company seem inevitable now, but they met with a great deal of skepticism, even though they had a good pitch right from the start. They had been inspired by natural brand pioneers like Aveda, which had created demand for natural products in the hair care market, and their elevator pitch was that they were "Aveda for the Home." That was compelling enough to draw some attention from potential backers, but ultimately people just couldn't believe these two guys with no experience at all in the cleaning products business could take on the big brands like Proctor and Gamble. The green market still seemed to have appeal only among do-gooders willing to put up with substandard products. As for their argument about setting themselves apart with quality design, when it came to washing hands and doing dishes, they were told consumers only cared about function and price, not aesthetics.

They weren't going to be able to raise any funding up front, so to create their first line they relied on a great deal of borrowed expertise, convincing lawyers, accountants, and suppliers to work for equity rather than cash. Looking back on those days, Eric reflects, "The essential skill at this stage is to infect others with your vision and passion. Make your mission contagious so that others will take the risk to work with you for very little up-front."

The first major piece of hustling they pulled off was to line up a chemist to help them craft their formulas. Adam had been mixing up batches of cleaners in their apartment, experimenting with all natural ingredients. The place was full of beer pitchers labeled "DON'T DRINK." Eventually he landed on some formulas that he was pretty happy with, but he realized he should bring in a professional.

Meanwhile Eric worked on branding and design, convincing a local graphic designer to create labels for them in return for equity As soon as the formulas were ready, they had labels printed and decided to go ahead with making some product. After six months of work they had a product line, but nowhere to sell. Now the real hustling began.

They started going door-to-door, calling on independently owned grocery stores, just showing up early in the morning and giving a 30-second pitch. The first store that placed an order was Mollie Stone's Market in Burlingham, California. For the next couple of months they drove around in Adam's mom's car to every independent grocery store in the San Francisco area. Before long Method was in 30 stores across the bay area. They hand-delivered the inventory to the stores.

They knew they needed to see the inventory selling if they wanted to stay in those stores and have any hope of selling to the chain stores, so they conducted a great deal of in-store marketing, which also allowed them to gain first-hand customer insights as well as learning the ins and outs of the grocery store business. Their efforts started to pay off in sales.

They were almost running out of the money they'd invested, though, and they needed to start to scale up soon by selling bigger orders to chains of stores if they had any hope of surviving. Now equipped with actual sales data showing proof of concept, they thought they'd be able to get meetings with bigger chains, but they wouldn't be able to fulfill larger orders with their current operation. They'd have to scale up on inventory before getting those orders, and they needed to put a proper distribution system in place—they couldn't sell to chains out of the back of a station wagon. But all of that would cost money they didn't have.

So they decided to pursue angel investments from anyone they could convince to believe in them, which turned out to be friends and family. They look back at this friends and family round as a great help not only financially, but in terms of motivation. "Many entrepreneurs struggle with the decision to take money from close friends and loved ones," Eric says. "The reality is that you don't have much of a choice. Before you've proven your idea, the only thing people can bet on is you, and, inevitably, the only people willing to do that are your friends and family. Of course, the upside to taking money from the people you care about most is that it puts lots of pressure on your back. You go from not wanting to let yourself down to not wanting to let your family down. It forces you to do everything you can to avoid sitting down at Christmas dinner saying, 'Sorry, Grandma, I lost that $10 thousand you loaned me.' "

After a small friends and family round of funding, they were able to hit their next big milestone by selling to the Ralph's chain in Southern California and QFC in Seattle. They had grown from being in 30 stores to 200, and they were making fairly good money, but they were burning through cash at a much faster rate than it was coming in. This is one of the most difficult challenges to manage: getting your cost of sales low enough and your volume of sales high enough to assure a profit. They now desperately needed more cash, so they decided to pursue venture capital. But not one firm wanted to back them.

Now they began wracking up serious credit card debt, eventually putting $100,000 on their cards. And if the stress of the debt wasn't bad enough, Eric's girlfriend dumped him. But that wasn't the worst of things: they spent many nights waking up in a cold sweat, fretting about how to pay back the money not only on their cards, but that they had borrowed from their friends and family. Their vendors began putting them on credit holds, which was going to force them to freeze production. They decided to scramble to find a bridge investment.

Things were so desperate that when they got into a car accident, they considered it a stroke of luck. They had just $16 left in the bank at the time, and the insurance payout allowed them to cover rent and food for a few months.

Then they managed to secure a bridge loan from a major gambling company in Las Vegas, and that gave them a leg up in finally securing their first bit of venture capital.

They now made some headway by getting into some regional chains, but they continued to burn through cash. Just a month after they'd found themselves flush with cash they were back to the cash-strapped life. They had to raise more capital. They lined up another series of pitches to potential investors, and landed their first really sizeable check, from a pair of venture capitalist brothers, for $500,000. They considered that a huge milestone, which warranted a proper celebration, and when they went out for a big celebration dinner, their credit card was declined. Fortunately they knew the owner and got off with an IOU.

The venture firm had promised them another $500,000 if they could get into 800 stores within 90 days. That meant expanding 400 percent in that time, a near-impossible task. But they went into hustle overdrive and cleared everything but sales pitching off their plates, competing furiously with each other to see how many sales they could rack up. Miraculously they hit their target in the nick of time.

They couldn't get off the burn-rate treadmill, and they knew it was time to swing for the fences by landing a national chain store account. There was only one national chain on their list: the one that stood for style and worked with such high-end designers as Todd Oldham and Michael Graves to bring style to the mass market at affordable prices—Target. They had tried to get into Target for some time to no avail, and then finally a friend of a friend, who had an unrelated meeting with the head buyer at Target, agreed to let them tag along to the meeting and make a quick pitch for Method at the end.

They had their dream meeting, and they were feeling confident, but as they describe the outcome, "Our chances were less than those of a snowball in hell. At least, that's how Target's divisional head put it after a cursory look at our presentation materials. He said our product was ordinary and our brand wouldn't have broad appeal. After weeks psyching ourselves up, we couldn't believe our ears. The buyer seemed annoyed with us for wasting his time."

They had stepped up to the plate and had struck out big time. Lots of founders would have been demoralized, and they were for a time, but they rallied. They had pulled off some amazing hustling, but they were about to manage a truly extraordinary feat. They decided they had to heed the response of the Target buyer and come up with a more stunning product, and that would come from a truly breakout design.

One of their design heroes was Karim Rashid, one of the most respected product designers in the world, whose work is in the collections of a number of museums. He was very interested in design democracy, bringing top design to mass-production products. Adam and Eric had been following his career for a while and had gone to see a few talks he had given. Now they decided to reach out to him.

Eric just sent him an email one day, appealing to Rashid's concern about design democracy. He wrote: "Karim, we want to reinvent an icon that sits on the current top of every sink in America, and we want you to do it." Karim thought it was an intriguing proposition. He'd never designed a product that you could buy for $3. So, to Adam and Eric's surprise, he accepted the offer.

Enlisting star power like that isn't cheap, though, and with their cash reserves so tight, they had to get Karim to agree to special terms. They negotiated a deal with him for a mix of cash up front and stock. Now they had a star name behind their product, and suddenly they were more attractive.

When a friend of Eric's offered to get them a meeting with the head of marketing at Target, they jumped at the opportunity. They'd be making an end run around the head buyer, but they figured if you can't get in through the front door, sometimes you have to climb through the window. As soon as the head of marketing heard Karim was on board, the meeting was booked. Target had been drooling over Karim for a while. Target did not want Method. Target wanted Karim, and Method was along for the ride.

This was the Hail-Mary pass for Method. Their model would either succeed or fail with this meeting, and they were going all in. The pressure was enormous, and Rashid's bowling pin-shaped soap bottle arrived just before the meeting. Eric filled the bottle with soap on the way to the presentation.

Increasing the tension, who did he see when he walked into the meeting? The head buyer, who had shot down their idea in the last Target meeting, was sitting in the room with his arms folded glaring at Eric. He did not look amused. As Eric gave his presentation, the head buyer cast a cloud over the room. No one gave any signals about how the pitch was going, and Eric thought he was bombing. Finally he unveiled the new bottle and passed it around the room, and as the head buyer picked it up and squeezed a stream of soap, he exclaimed, "Oh my God! Even I would use this!" The next thing Eric knew they had a deal for Target to test the product line in 100 stores in the Chicago and San Francisco areas. If they hit the sales target, they would get their coveted national distribution.

The only problem now was that the product needed to be on the shelves in three months. As Eric and Adam talked, their excitement turned to dread. The bottle they'd shown in the meeting was just a prototype, and even if it was put into production that moment, it didn't seem possible they could make that deadline. They had to hustle big time yet again.

That very evening Adam jumped on the redeye to Chicago to meet with their head of production. The two begged and cajoled and called in favors all around Chicago. If somebody wouldn't return their call, they would show up in person to plead the case. Remarkably, they were able to meet the deadline.

By August 2002, Method was on the shelves in Target's test markets, and the initial consumer response was encouraging. Customers were writing in praise of the product and asking if the company could make an all-natural shampoo or laundry detergent. But at the same time, problems were starting to emerge in the stores. For one thing, customers were picking up and opening the bottles to smell the liquid and to try to figure out how the unusual bottle worked, which was making a mess on the shelves. Sales began to fall.

So the guys hit the stores, cleaning up the mess, handing out coupons, and schmoozing managers. They even resorted to buying the product off the shelves in some stores and giving it away in the parking lots to try to lure customers. None of their efforts reversed the drop in sales, though, and they missed their sales target. That seemed the end. But as is the case in so many stories of successful startups, they were about to get a remarkable lucky break.

A new buyer took over the category at Target and she liked the Method products. She had reviewed the numbers and believed the sales target had been set too high. She had also determined that Method was bringing in a more premium customer to the stores and was driving greater overall profitability. So Method was going national after all. That was the break that finally got them out of their burn-rate dilemma and they were off the treadmill and running.

SIMPLE AND SINCERE CAN WORK WONDERS

Charles Best was teaching during the day and working on building DonorsChoose.org in the evening, essentially working two fulltime jobs. He didn't want to leave the classroom and be just another Ivy League graduate who teaches for two years and then takes off. And staying in the classroom had several important benefits in growing the organization: he was able to run the operation out of his classroom, he continued making a salary so he didn't risk personal bankruptcy, and being a teacher gave him credibility both with teachers and the media.

Teachers are approached all the time with new ideas to help them in the classroom, but they're usually cooked up by people with no teaching experience. The media loved the story of a teacher in the Bronx taking this initiative all on his own. One last benefit of continuing to teach was that he had access to an energetic work force that required no pay: his students. Charles's first promotional effort was a letter-writing campaign that they made possible.

Charles got hold of the mailing lists for both his high school and college alumni networks, and his students volunteered every day after school for about three months, writing 2,000 letters by hand and mailing them out. Charles remembers, "My classroom became a postal distribution center." The campaign generated $30,000 in donations to projects and was exactly the kick-start Charles needed to move the site forward.

The power of an old-fashioned analog letter is often overlooked in our digital age. Charles made letter writing central to his model. Right from the first 11 projects funded, the teachers had students write thank-you letters and took photographs of the projects in action to go with them. They even enclosed copies of receipts showing how the money was used so that donors could see the impact. This was a different type of philanthropy, transparent and with a personal touch.

Donations grew steadily, but Charles was stretching himself too thin. "There was a point in year two," he says, "where the work load was becoming too much to handle, and I had actually decided to shut down if we didn't get an angel investment that would enable me to hire one staff member to handle the operations." Once again, Charles hustled. He got a directory of 100 foundations, and went down the list cold calling them, leaving voicemails. Out of 100 calls, only one called him back, but it was a good one, the Goldman Sachs Foundation. They decided to make a small grant to enable him to hire the staff member. This was about three weeks before Charles's self-imposed deadline. This one break allowed Charles to stick with the cause, improving the web site and scaling up outreach.

KEY TAKEAWAYS

Every founder has to be willing to be a salesperson, and pitching of one kind or another takes up a great deal of time. This is especially true in the early days, but the job of selling the vision is never done. And the work can't just be farmed out. In story after story of successful launches, the fine line between success and failure comes down to that one last pitch, an apparently hare-brained idea, and the leveraging of any and all personal connections. And the founder generally has no idea when that lucky break will come.

Founders must not be hesitant to mobilize friends and family, and though some people are understandably reluctant to borrow money from this network—which is by no means necessary—in many cases it provides the basis for gaining traction. But money is only one means of driving momentum: founders must also leverage the resources of people's time and passion. I have never met a successful entrepreneur who is not a hustler.

Hustle will look different depending on the industry, product, market, and context, but it boils down to selling a vision of the future, inviting people into that vision, and making them feel an integral contributor to it.

1. Sell the Vision

The vision for your organization may take a while to come fully into focus, and the pitching process can be a vital part of bringing clarity. People are sure to share all kinds of responses, including utter skepticism. They're likely to give you a host of reasons that you should abandon the effort. But they will likely also share some great ideas for efforts to try and changes to make in your plan.

Selling your vision takes both a great deal of resilience and a great deal of passion. A key factor in getting buy-in is persuasively making the case for how your product or service will improve people's lives and will introduce a superior model. This is one way in which being innovative provides an edge: key potential support-ers want to know that they can help to make substantial change happen. The bolder your ambition, and the more convincing your vision, the more enthusiastically people from your own family to those you cold call to the major funding organizations will come onboard.

Key Question: How will the world be different if we are successful?

2. Invite Co-Creators

The social innovator cannot bring her vision to life alone, she must invite co-creators into the process. Contributions from others with the necessary expertise or connections, often given voluntarily or for no cash up front and some portion of equity in the future, are often the key factors in getting through the gauntlet of the building phase. Founders must be constantly thinking about how others might assist them and be willing to reach out to whoever it is they think can solve the problems they're facing. Even the most improbable of requests may be agreed to, especially if the founder is able to help others to achieve their own goals. Aspiring social innovators should never underestimate how many people would like to be a part of solving the problems.

Key Question: How will others benefit from helping you make your vision into a reality?

CHAPTER FOUR

Fund Through Commitment

Raising funds is one of the most challenging and time-consuming jobs for every founder, whether of a for-profit or non-profit organization. As we saw with the story of Method, this may be true even if a product is gaining substantial sales. As we saw with Charity: Water, the same can be true even if the organization is creating strong impact.

The purely for-profit model presents its own distinctive challenges. As high-profile for-profit purpose-driven companies like Ben & Jerry's, Burt's Bees, Patagonia, Whole Foods, Method, and Warby Parker have reaped such rewards and have proven the concept, there is no question that the concept of social impact investing has gained traction. A growing cadre of investors is looking to put their money into companies that can come through with both a solid financial return on investment (ROI) and a social return on investment (SROI), which is the social and/or environmental impact of the organization. But this in no way means that money is easy to attract, or that satisfying these investors is any less difficult than pleasing those looking primarily for quick returns. In many cases, it may be more difficult due to the added variables that come into play when looking for financial, social, and environmental performance.

When it comes to finding investors for social enterprises, the investor and the social entrepreneur must be in clear agreement about the expected outcomes in terms of profit and purpose. The pursuit of purpose can be (but is not necessarily) at odds with the maximization of profits, and this can result in a long-term power struggle between investors and the social entrepreneur.

Not every investor is right for every deal. Investors come in all shapes and sizes and are hoping for various types of returns. Some influential investors are strong supporters of pursuing a triple bottom line, and others argue that it's fundamentally flawed.

PROMOTING A NEW VERSION OF CAPITALISM

One strong supporter of the social innovation cause in the investment community is Albert Wenger, a partner at Union Square Ventures, who has invested in some of the most successful tech companies including Twitter and Tumblr. He considers himself a pure tech venture capitalist, not an impact investor, and yet he is strongly in favor of the social enterprise. He argues that while the current version of capitalism has been incredibly efficient with technical innovation, creating and distributing everything from computers to clothing at cheaper and cheaper prices and to an ever-widening market, it has been inadequate in solving the largest social problems. "The problem of technological innovation is not the primary problem that we still need to solve," he says. "The primary problems now are the very large-scale ones: giving people access to good education, quality healthcare, poverty alleviation, and not destroying our planet." He argues that we must usher in a new version of capitalism that will shift the focus from purely techno-logical innovation to social innovation.

One key problem with the current version of capitalism that Wenger points to is *short-termism*: the mandate to produce short-term shareholder returns has led to the neglect of longer-term vision and strategy, and it leads stakeholders to attempt to extract value from organizations too soon. A good example of this, according to Mr. Wenger, is the Myspace acquisition. "News Corp. bought it, and paid what they thought was a reasonably high price for it and then proceeded to want to recover that price very quickly. So they tried to monetize the network very, very heavily, ultimately contributing to its collapse."

Even an organization's managers may only work at the company for five or ten years, and investors are generally looking to exit even more quickly. This fundamental disconnect between the incentives for short-term profit maximization and long-term value creation is one of the most difficult challenges for any for-profit firm, but it can be especially difficult for a social enterprise given the tension between the pursuit of purpose and that of profit that they're also struggling with. Wenger stresses that "In a social enterprise, management, directors, and shareholders must set a long-term vision for the health of their company and make those decisions that align with those goals without the interference of short-term focused shareholders."

WHEN PROFIT TRUMPS PURPOSE

Another influential investor, David S. Rose, an angel investor and entrepreneur who has founded or funded more than 75 companies, makes a different argument about the challenge of building social enterprise. He insists that you cannot create a successful company if you're trying to pursue purpose and profit simultaneously. When the rubber meets the road, you must choose either profit or purpose, he says. "It's wonderful to think that one can have one's cake and eat it too," he argues. "In the real world, however, things tend to optimize in one area. It is nearly impossible to try and truly optimize for a double bottom-line. Starting a new venture is insanely tough. It's really, really difficult. Given the fact that the majority of new businesses fail even though entrepreneurs are busting their rear ends to try and make them succeed only economically, to overlay on top of that a secondary goal is really, really challenging."

He believes in doing good through business, he just believes the only way to do that is to give clear priority to profit over purpose. In fact, he has invested in, and serves as the chairman of the board for Porti Familia—a company bringing modern healthcare to the slums of Lima, Peru—a company that is certainly doing a great deal of good in the world. Other investors in the company include some of the biggest impact investment funds in the world, such as Acumen and respons-Ability. Rose says, "We all agree that the company is doing good things, but I invested in it not to do good things—I can give money to charity for that. I invested in this company to make money, and oh, by the way, it's making money in a good way by doing good things."

THE BENEFITS OF THE BENEFIT CORPORATION

One way to try to assure that those who invest in your organization are in alignment with your mission is to organize as a benefit corporation. A benefit corporation is a new class of corporation created for social entrepreneurs. It has two distinctive attributes. First, the purpose of the organization is to pursue positive financial, social, and environmental impact. Second, benefit corporations have increased transparency and accountability on social and environmental performance.

Ron Cordes, one of the leaders in the impact investing movement, has had a long career in investment, including serving as co-Chairman for the $21 billion asset management firm Genworth, explains the rationale behind the benefit corporation well. He points out that most investment rounds include multiple investors and, more often than not, the investors have never met each other; they're just names on a capitalization table. There is no way to understand the other investors' motives for making their investments. Typically, to align investors around a common mission, the CEO of the company must bring a group of them together.

Incorporating as a benefit corporation sends a clear signal to investors that they are signing on to your profit and purpose goals. "You have the goals in writing," he says, "baked into the articles." Inevitably, a company will run into challenging circumstances as it grows, Cordes notes. "Growing a business is never a linear path. It's always two steps forward, one step back. And crashes like 2008 happen," he added. When setbacks occur, he explains, investor support for the social and environmental mission of a company may wane, and a company may face strong pressure to put the mission aside. "Things like that can happen," says Cordes. "If the values are not codified, you're going to be relying on the collective good intentions of the group."

THE TRUE COST OF FREE MONEY

Because of the challenges involved in dealing with investors, one might be more inclined to pursue purely philanthropic funding. But philanthropic funders present their own challenges. Though philanthropic capital may seem free, there is a high cost to that free money.

The cost of philanthropic capital can be much higher than that of commercial capital. The cost that often goes unaccounted for is the time required. Many of the executive directors I speak with regularly spend 40 percent or more of their time in any given week fundraising. Most of that time investment, either by the executive director or by the development staff, has no guaranteed pay off. It's very common to spend 20 hours on a detailed grant application and not win the grant. And in the situations where the organization is successful at winning the grant, they often have to dedicate precious staff time to monitoring and reporting impact back to the donor. Time is the key cost of philanthropic capital. Time spent on constant fundraising is time not being spent on strategies and tactics for improving service to serve the beneficiaries. So, due to the constant chase for money, the services to beneficiaries often suffer.

Philanthropic capital also often comes with its own form of strings attached. A donor may want to fund a project that is not exactly in alignment with the core mission of the organization. But because funds are needed, the conditions are accepted, and an organization drifts away from its original mission. In addition, most philanthropists have no appetite for failure; they only want to fund a program that is proven. Thus, many charitable organizations are unwilling to take risks for fear that they may be criticized for failures and jeopardize their own funding sources. Philanthropic capital disincentives risk.

As Charity: Water's Scott Harrison says, "In the for-profit world, I think you can break things a little more easily, because it's not donor money. You can completely burn through $5 million and realize, 'that didn't work'. We (nonprofits) have a different kind of stewardship and accountability. In the traditional startup world you could try five things and you only need one to work. If we try five things, we kind of need all five to work."

Krista Donaldson of D-Rev also stresses how this can stifle the experimentation that is so crucial to innovation. "The traditional nonprofit operation depends on a strategic plan and the investment of a lot of resources in one big effort. It is very hard to change direction. For the most part, if you fail at your mission, very few funders are going to say, 'okay, here, let me give you the same amount of money or more to go try something new.'

In consideration of all of these challenges, this chapter will introduce a number of ingenious funding models that have been developed, many by the founders profiled in the book, which every founder and organization should consider. At the core of the success of all of these techniques is that the founders were able to convince funders, whether investors, donors, or consumers, about the authenticity of their commitment to the purpose and the quality of the product or service, and in turn they inspired the authentic and engaged commitment of funders. Crucial to solving the funding conundrum is finding investors and donors who are committed to the same cause and vision that drives you.

SMART CROWDFUNDING

A hot new fundraising approach that has emerged in recent years is crowdfunding—raising small amounts of capital from a large number of people, typically through an online platform.

Soma founder Mike Del Ponte knows a thing or two about crowdfunding and executed a brilliant fundraising campaign by blending a smart mix of angel investment and crowdfunding on Kickstarter.com to launch his company. The most successful crowdfunding campaigns have been launched at the design phase, when an organization has created a good prototype of a product, but requires capital to go into full production. This was true for Soma, and Mike not only did a great job of attracting funds through his Kickstarter campaign, he also leveraged it to help draw in traditional investors.

The key to successful crowdfunding is mobilizing both friends and the media. The media needs to be well targeted, with strong readership, a large reach, and a relevant audience. But potentially more important than the media is getting your friends excited and on board as advocates. In order to do this, you've got to spend a lot of time prior to launch soliciting and listening to their advice, giving them a sense of ownership in your mission, which increases their commitment to seeing it succeed. Surprisingly, Mike found that crowdfunding is not only about the money you raise in the campaign, it's about the media exposure and about building a community and gaining social proof of concept. One last benefit is that it helps you learn what consumers want from your product. Mike used his campaign to capitalize on all of these benefits.

Mike had never imagined he would end up running a high-design, sustainable products company; he had planned on being a priest. As a student at Boston College, a Jesuit-Catholic university, he was inspired by the priests and nuns there to follow in their footsteps. So he headed next to divinity school at Yale, where he discovered that while he didn't think he'd make a great priest, he was good at inspiring and connecting people to empower people to follow their dreams. He also met a group of young social entrepreneurs at the school, and he started helping them out with their ventures and discovered he really liked it. So he became a social entrepreneur himself and launched Sparkseed when he was 24. Sparkseed is an organization aimed at helping young social entrepreneurs gain access to capital, mentorship, conferences, and community—everything they would need to make their organization thrive. But after running the organization for a number of years, launching initiatives around the globe—including food programs in Africa, composting programs in the United States, and helping design green companies—he decided he wanted to get some experience in the for-profit startup sector. So he joined a young startup called Branchout.com, a professional network on Facebook, where he led the marketing team. While he was there, the user base grew to 25 million and the company raised $49 million in venture capital. But he felt that as interesting as the work was, it wasn't his calling.

Then one night when he was throwing a dinner party at his home, a friend asked for a glass of water. When Mike grabbed his "leading brand" water filter pitcher out of the fridge, he was struck by the black specks floating in the water, and by how ugly and ungainly the cheap plastic pitcher was. He certainly couldn't bring it out to his nicely set dinner table. So he decided to pour the filtered water into a glass wine decanter. Which was how he found his Purpose Point. He was passionate about the water crisis, and had followed what Charity: Water was doing closely. An idea hit him: why doesn't somebody make a water filter that's beautiful, that works well, and that also does good? He decided he wanted to disrupt the water-purification industry with a product that consumers could be proud of on both an aesthetic and a moral level.

That fateful dinner party was the genesis for what *Fast Company* called "The best design story of the year," and Soma was named one of *Inc. Magazine's* top 25 Most Audacious Companies.

To move Soma from the concept to the prototype phase, they initially raised an angel round of $1.2 million from Silicon Valley luminaries like Tim Ferris and Michael Birch. They had a great response and had to turn investors away. The round closed in the summer of 2012.

KICKSTART

After that round closed they began to focus on their Kickstarter campaign, which launched in December 2012. Mike set a goal of $100,000 for their campaign. Mike and a couple of virtual assistants got together to launch the Kickstarter campaign.

Mike didn't want to leave anything to chance, so he interviewed 15 of the top-earning Kickstarter creators. Their projects ranged from a grizzly bear jacket to a gaming console that raised nearly $8.6 million on Kickstarter. According to Mike, "What we learned is that whether you're successful or struggling, your Kickstarter campaign is often '40 days of chaos,' as one creator put it." Either you succeed beyond your wildest dreams and are overwhelmed with inquiries from backers, press, retailers, and investors, or you struggle to achieve your goal and frantically beg bloggers and friends to spread the word. Either type of overwhelm can be a huge headache.

Soma did not have a huge staff. The team included three full-time teammates, two virtual assistants, one intern, and an army of friends. The network of friends had a strong sense of ownership because they were engaged months before the Kickstarter launched. So they got creative, used virtual assistants, and laid out a clear strategy to hit their goals. Mike learned some lessons in the process.

Mike says, "Chefs don't prepare meals like you and me. They don't start 15 to 60 minutes before dinner. Instead, they prep everything in advance (sometimes days before), so they can just heat the food and make it look nice when it's time to eat. This concept was critical to our success. We did 90 percent of the work in advance."

In order to get people to fund your Kickstarter project, you first have to get them to the project's site. But, not all traffic is created equal. Some traffic is more likely to yield backers than others. Soma's virtual assistants analyzed the traffic for successful Kickstarter campaigns and they found that the top drivers of traffic were:

- Facebook
- Direct traffic (primarily via email)
- Twitter
- Kickstarter
- Blogs

Based on this data, they decided to focus all of their attention on just two goals: first, getting coverage on the right blogs, and second, activating their networks to create buzz on Facebook, Twitter, and email. Mike looked for the following characteristics when compiling their media list:

- Relevance—will their readers LOVE your project?
- Readership—how much traffic does their site get?
- Reach—will the blog reach prospective backers by promoting your post via email newsletter, RSS feed, Facebook, Twitter, or other channels?
- Relationship—Do you know anybody there? When they pitched a blogger without a relationship, less than 1 percent

even responded. With introductions, their success rate was more than 50 percent.

They compiled their media list outreach, complete with a dossier for each property, and had the virtual assistants reach out to each property. Once they connected with a blogger who was interested in covering their project, they didn't send them some canned email, but tailored it specifically to that publication and made it as easy as possible for them to write a piece on Soma. Bloggers have to pump out a ton of stories, so make it easy on them and valuable to their readers.

Once they landed the story, they pushed to get confirmation on the timing of the piece. You want to ensure each story reaches people who will back your project. So after a story is confirmed, they pushed to try to time the piece with the launch of the campaign.

They got a good deal of coverage in just 10 days (*Forbes, Fast Company, Inc.*, Mashable, Cool Hunting, Business Insider, *GOOD*, Salon, Gear Patrol, Thrillist, The Huffington Post, and many more). In order to understand how the press impacted the campaign, one week into the Kickstarter campaign they reviewed their press coverage. Surprisingly, the post that earned the most money was on a site most people have never heard of: www.good.is, the online property of *GOOD* magazine.

Mike says, "We stopped and asked ourselves, 'why did good.is outperform bigger and more well-known media outlets?' We discovered that good.is was in some cases ten times more valuable than other press because the audience is relevant, the readership is substantial (400,000+ unique monthly visitors), we got an introduction to a writer at *GOOD*, and we reached prospective backers through *GOOD*'s daily email and its Facebook and Twitter accounts."

But most importantly, Mike says that the reason they were successful is because of their friends. He asked for (and listened to) his friends' advice. They asked for feedback on everything from the company's name to product design to pricing. He offered them "sneak peeks" that no one else gets. They showed their friends product renderings, pictures, and the Kickstarter video long before they were released to the public. Letting friends in on the process and allowing them to give input gives them a sense of ownership, and they are more apt to advocate on your behalf.

They threw a launch party. "Having a large group of people in one room, all excited about your project, creates a united energy you can't create through emails, phone calls, or one-on-one meetings," says Mike. They invited more than 50 motivated and influential friends, showed them the Kickstarter video and made a speech telling them why the company needs their help and exactly what they need them to do. The people who attended their launch party ended up being their first backers and their most passionate evangelists.

This clear strategy paid off. Soma quickly became one of the most popular projects on Kickstarter and was featured as a "popular project," which then engaged people browsing Kickstarter searching for cool projects to back. Within only nine days, they hit their goal of $100,000 and ended up raising $150,000, one and a half times their goal, throughout the entire campaign.

FOLLOW-ON FUNDING

"Crowdfunding is not just about the money," according to Mike. "If you were asking about the five best things about crowdfunding, money would be at the bottom of the list." As the field of crowdfunding is maturing, more people are realizing that the benefits of crowdfunding extend far beyond money.

Crowdfunding builds community. Gathering a group of people around the goal of getting the project funded creates the core of your community. The backers are the early adopters of a brand and the best advocates. They are the ones Mike hopes will buy Soma water filters for their friends for the holidays.

Crowdfunding is great for market research. You can test out messaging and pricing, send out surveys to them, and meet with them to understand who your audience actually is. From there you can build archetypes of your customers.

Crowdfunding also builds social proof prior to launch. Most companies launch without any proof of acceptance by the market, with no way to know if consumers will respond. But due to Soma's success on Kickstarter, they had already been ranked number one on *Fast Company*'s list of top design stories and were named one of the top 25 most audacious companies by *Inc. Magazine*. The market was responding.

They had run a successful Kickstarter campaign, but in the scheme of their financial needs, $150,000 was fairly minimal. They had already raised $1.7 million, and needed to raise another $2.5 million. So they honed their pitch and went back in for another round of financing.

The investors in this round were impressed by the Kickstarter success, it had turned a lot of heads in Silicon Valley, but they prudently noted that a one-month prelaunch campaign is not a business model.

When approaching the second-round investors, Mike used the success of the Kickstarter campaign, but was careful to put it in context. He says, "The customer insights that we had were equally or more impressive than the money we made on Kickstarter because the amount of money raised on Kickstarter in the timeframe was relatively small. There is one month out of hopefully decades-long life of a company, and it is $150,000, out of what will hopefully be a billion dollar company. So we stated that upfront, and said, we did the Kickstarter. We wanted to get proof of concept, and our goal was $100,000. We did $150,000. Thousands of people signed up, and we are thankful for that. But here is the road map of how to really build the company. Kickstarter was one very early milestone that definitely presented the customer insights. That was incredibly impressive, because most companies pre-launch don't know that much about the customers."

Going through the fundraising process the second round was different than the first round. This time they had a business to run while they were raising money, so they wanted to do it very efficiently in order to not disrupt the momentum of their business.

Mike sat down with the lead investor from Soma's first round and brainstormed who should be the second round. The name that emerged at the top of the list was Kirsten Green of Forerunner Ventures. Mike said, "Forerunner is fantastic at e-commerce. They have invested in and helped grow some of the coolest e-commerce companies like Bonobos, Warby Parker, and Birchbox. The second thing is that Kristen is an absolute hustler for her portfolio companies. She is very proactive about asking where she could help. She has great ideas and right off the bat we knew that she would be a great partner. She and Forerunner in general add so much value." They met her and immediately saw the value that she would add and her excitement about Soma. They wanted to lead the second round and Soma was excited to have them do so.

Next, they circled back with their original investors and gave them the opportunity to reinvest. Then they let it be known that they were raising another round of capital, and other investors jumped into the round. So much so that Soma had to turn away investors.

They closed their $2.5 million round by the middle of the summer of 2013 and were back to work equipped with more cash and expertise to help them launch a successful company.

Soma raised money both from a crowd-funding campaign on Kickstarter as well as through a traditional seed round. This hybrid seed-crowd round is a new approach to raising early stage capital. So why did Mike choose that fundraising strategy?

Mike originally was just planning to raise a seed round from investors. He didn't like the idea of crowdfunding because he wasn't sure that great brands could be launched on Kickstarter. There are plenty of cool projects launched on the site, but not many examples of lasting brands.

Secondly, the amount of effort required to run a successful campaign does not match the amount of capital raised. They raised $3.7 million in the more traditional fashion, and they spent much more energy to raise $150,000 on Kickstarter. $150,000 in proportion isn't a significant proportion of fundraising.

Mike said the reason why he chose to raise a seed-crowd round was that "Great advisors emphasized the benefits of crowdfunding as proof of concept. We de-risk our business by proving that thousands of people would pull out their credit cards and purchase Soma at the product pitch stage. A lot of companies will spend a ton of money bringing a product to market, cross their fingers, and hope that it does well. We had a significant proof point earlier on in the stage of the company."

Applying the seed-crowd strategy allows a company to raise a level of capital that is unlikely to be raised on a crowdfunding platform, while simultaneously proving the concept of a product prelaunch.

GOING TO THE WELL

After Scott Harrison raised the $1 million from Michael Birch to support operations, he and the team had some breathing room to figure out how to make the 100 percent funding-model work. He came up with an idea that has brilliantly solved the operations funding dilemma, inspired by some prescient advice from a savvy CEO.

Scott was in a meeting fundraising for operations from some CEOs. At that time they were spending $100,000 per month on operations. Somebody spoke up and asked, "What if you get 100 people to commit to giving $1,000 per month?" Scott thought about it. Twelve thousand dollars a year is not too big of a commitment, many people in New York spend that per month on rent. All he would have to do was convince 100 people and they would have all of their ops covered annually. Scott said, "So we started to ask people for twelve grand a year, and they started saying yes!"

The first person that signed on for this regular giving was Shawn Budde, a member of their board at the time. Then others began to follow. Scott was in a meeting with the CEO of Saks Fifth Avenue and he committed to two thousand dollars a month, but he said, "Make us all sign up for a three-year commitment, that way you can properly plan for the future." So, from there forward, they asked for every donor to commit to giving for the next three years. In addition to Michael Birch's initial donation of $1 million, he also committed to giving $5,000 per month. So, now there were different levels of giving—$1,000, $2,000, and $5,000 per month—and everybody was signing up for three-year commitments.

The team decided that they needed to call this group of recurring donors something. They wanted to create a community. So, Vic came up with the idea of referring to them as "The Well." The hope is that the well never runs dry.

Thus far it hasn't. In 2012, Charity: Water spent $5.5 million on operations, but the well raised $11 million. Not only are they surviving, but they are getting ahead and are able to make prudent financial-planning decisions, such as hiring and office expansion.

For the third year they were trying to think about ways to scale the party. They thought, "this year let's ask everybody to stay home." Instead of coming to a party, why not ask everybody to give up their birthday? Scott thought he'd take the lead and see if it caught on, "I'm going to give up my birthday party this year. I'll ask my friends to donate my age in dollars. I was turning 32. Everybody I know has $32 they could give to charity; they would have spent that on a cab and a tip to the waitress on any given night."

So Vik created an HTML page. Scott wrote a mission statement about giving up his birthday, promising that he'd go to drill a well himself in Kenya with their money if the campaign was successful. The campaign was successful and they didn't spend a dime or any energy to plan and host an event. Scott celebrated his birthday in Kenya drilling a well, which was streamed live for the whole world to see.

Along with Scott, Charity: Water put out a call for all September birthdays to give up their birthday. Ninety-two people joined in, and they raised a total of $150,000 from the birthday campaign. In year one, they made $15,000 from the party, year two jumped tenfold to $150,000. The following year they set an ambitious goal for September, they wanted to dig 333 wells in Ethiopia. That year they raised $1.5 million. Each year they had seen a ten-fold growth in their September fundraising.

The idea was more powerful than they could have imagined. It worked well for a number of reasons. First of all, it just redirected spending that would have been occurring for birthday gifts in the first place. It's easier to give to charity than to find a present for someone, and it feels better. So, it's an easy ask from the person whose birthday it is. Also, the idea of asking for the amount of dollars to align with your birthday turned out to be an incredibly sticky idea.

The team thought that there was something bigger that they could do with this idea of giving up your birthday. So, the next year, they launched My: Charity: Water—a customizable web platform that allows an individual to set a fundraising goal and reach out to her friends and family to meet that goal.

Then people started getting more creative with it and using the platform for more than just birthdays. One guy ran a campaign called "Save my beard/Shave my beard." He encouraged his friends and family to tell him what he should do with his beard. Each donation was a vote toward whether you wanted to save or shave his beard, and whichever side raised the most money would win. A member of the military in Afghanistan raised $1,000 by writing haikus for those that funded his campaign.

A beard contest? A soldier writing haikus? These are ideas that the Charity: Water team could have never thought of, but they are effective, authentic ways for individuals to tap into their networks, tell the story about the water crisis, and tell about how Charity: Water is trying to create a solution. The real power has come from letting their donors become storytellers. By empowering their donors, they have become brand ambassadors with a very easy way to engage their network and raise funds online.

EMBRACE 2.0

Since the purpose of the Embrace Warmer was to reduce infant mortality in developing countries, the founders assumed that the nonprofit structure would be the best choice for the organization. They thought they wouldn't be able to price for profit. But they still wanted to "operate as a business," as so many social entrepreneurs do. They planned to sell products and make a profit margin that would be reinvested in the business for growth.

A key question in their decision making was the source of funding. They thought that structuring as a nonprofit would allow them access to philanthropic capital—grassroots donations as well as grants—which they thought was necessary because as Jane recalls, "Given the inherent risk associated with what we were attempting to do (an untested management team bringing to market an unprecedented medical device) and the uncertainty of the commercial viability of the product, and given the type of customers we wanted to serve, we decided the best option was to go down the nonprofit route and created a 501(c)3."

They soon realized their naïveté on a number of levels. Jane says, "When I want a good laugh, I look at our first business plan. We projected that with two people and $100,000, we would be able to bring the product to market in one year." The team had little understanding of how much time, effort, and capital it would take to bring Embrace from concept to market. They also had no clue how much of their time would be dedicated to chasing after donor money. Jane estimates that up to 40 percent of their time was dedicated to fundraising—that's almost half of their time not spent on building a really great product, building out a distribution channel, or creating organizational infrastructure—but very inefficiently chasing down donors, which only resulted in a relatively low amount of money raised.

It's a common pitfall to think that nonprofit funding is free. It seems free, you just set up a nonprofit and ask for money. But the energy spent writing grants, submitting lengthy incubator applications, hosting events, running online fundraising campaigns, and the like all comes at a cost—your limited time. These activities shift the focus away from actually building a game-changing product or service. In addition, funders can ask you to slightly tweak your focus in order to fall within the guidelines of their grants. Most foundations like to fund programs that are already having an impact, they generally don't like funding research and design. Especially at the startup stages, an organization must trade impact for philanthropic money.

So, rather than continue in the nonprofit structure, they chose to take a bold structural move. Embrace spun out a for-profit in order to gain access to investment capital. So, Embrace was split into two separate, but related entities.

The nonprofit arm, Embrace, continued to hold the intellectual property it had already created during the concept and design phase, donate the product to the poorest communities through NGO partners, and build an ecosystem of services around baby health care. These activities would be funded by philanthropic capital and royalties from licensing the intellectual property.

The new for-profit entity, Embrace Innovations, licenses the intellectual property from the nonprofit under a revenue-sharing agreement, manufactures, conducts clinical testing and future R&D, and sets up the distribution and sales channels for the bottom of the pyramid market. This entity is funded by investment from social venture capitalists.

Jane describes the functional practicality of this set up. "This allows the for-profit entity to develop and focus its competencies to sell and distribute products, as well as to conduct research and development. At the same time, the nonprofit is able to focus on broader issues around newborn health, through training, education, and monitoring and evaluation. Early last year, we were able to close a Series-A round of financing from Khosla Impact Fund and Capricorn Investment Group, giving us a launch pad by which to try this new structure. Thus far, through this approach, Embrace and Embrace Innovations have helped more than 3,000 babies with our product. While our primary focus is in India, Embrace is doing pilot projects with NGO partners in 10 countries, and we hope to further scale this year."

Embrace wanted investors who believed in profit and purpose, so rather than approaching the traditional venture capital community, they focused on more impact-driven investors. They spoke with Acumen and Omidyar—two leaders in the field of impact investing. But they ended up working with funds that were a bit more profit focused, but still cared about impact. Khosla and Capricorn were two such funds, and they invested.

"Khosla himself has run a business before. So, he really understands the nuts and bolts of operations and also believes in impact. In fact, the first time I sat down with him, he asked me at the end 'If you had to choose one, what would it be? Making money or making impact.' I told him that if I had just wanted to make money, I would've done something else, other than Embrace. It was very clear to me when I answered him, but I told him, impact. If I had to choose one thing, it would be impact. Although to me the two actually go hand in hand, because if we want to scale this like crazy, then it has to be profitable."

VISION CAPITAL

Lerer Ventures is an investment firm that operates on a straight-forward assumption: any business that has not been disrupted by the Internet will be. They are always looking for David and Goliath stories, new companies that can tap the power of the Internet to disrupt an industry. When Ben Lerer, a partner at the firm and co-founder of Thrillist Media Group, met Neil and Dave of Warby Parker he saw just such an opportunity.

For Ben, a core criteria in investing in a for-purpose brand is authenticity; any social good that a company says it's promoting must be a matter of true commitment, not just marketing ploy. With Warby Parker, the impact of giving away a pair of glasses for every pair bought was perfectly clear, and the team had the expertise from Neil's five years working on the problem at VisionSpring to get it done. Ben was also impressed by the personal passion Neil brought to the cause and the commitment of those five years. "That said something about Neil and his character," says Ben.

It is easy to believe that investors make decisions purely on financial models but investors, especially venture capitalists, are investing in people, not spreadsheets. Ben's comments about the authenticity of the Warby Parker commitment to its mission speak powerfully to this point. If a social mission is genuine and comes from a place of authenticity, even though from a strictly profit and loss perspective it will probably cost more to run the business, the payoffs of the approach can far outweigh the losses. The success of Warby Parker shows that funding purpose with a totally for-profit model really is possible. It takes a really good product and a really authentic message. That winning strategy allowed the Warby Parker founders to raise substantial funding even though they were launch-ing in the wake of the 2008 financial crisis, which dried up so much investment money.

As Neil recalls, "The crisis of 2008 scared the crap out of all the banks. They overreacted, they would basically not lend to compa-nies that have less than two years of tax returns." They were a company that was financially solid from launch, lead by MBAs from one of the best business schools in the world, and they couldn't get a small business loan.

In order to get a simple $50,000 line of credit, they had to put $50,000 of their own dollars as collateral. They were borrowing their own money and paying interest for the pleasure of doing so. There was no other way for the company to build a credit history.

Then they went to 14 different banks and were turned down 14 times. The bank officers would tell say, "You have the best business plan we've ever seen, and the best performance in this short time that we've ever seen, but our hands are tied." Finally, through a family friend, a regional bank in New Jersey gave them a $200,000 term loan that was backed by the Small Business Administration. Even so, they still had to personally guarantee it and put up $100,000 of collateral. "We were really only borrowing like a $100,000," Neil said. "We had to sign all these crazy documents saying that we wouldn't use the money to build an aquarium or a zoo." The whole point of having the federal government guarantee small business loans is that if the business defaults, the SBA will pay the bank back 90 percent of the loan, but the bank still required 50 percent of the loan amount for collateral. Apparently the paperwork for the bank to recover that 90 percent in the event of failure is so onerous that they rarely do it.

So they jumped through all the hoops, put down $100,000 collateral, and promised not to build an aquarium or zoo with the money, just to get a $200,000 SBA-backed small business loan. They kept growing like crazy through the summer and fall of 2010, and needed more cash to continue to grow, so they raised a small $500,000 seed round of funding through a convertible debt from friends and a few angel investors.

In May 2011, 15 months after they launched, they set out to raise a $2.5 million round. In this first round, they had 46 investors. That is not a typo, 46 investors for a round of $2.5 million. From a traditional fundraising perspective, and from a purely logistical perspective, this is a nightmare.

But they decided to engage with this many investors for a reason. Neil explains their thinking, "Our thought was we've gotten this far because of all the good will of all these people. Why not get more people that are awesome." They were extremely deliberate in their search, targeting investors in tech, entertainment, and fashion. Within the tech world, Lerer Ventures led the round, and First Round Capital, SV Angel, and Thrive also invested. From the entertainment world they had Ashton Kutcher, Ryan Gosling, Troy Carter (Lady Gaga's manager), and Ariel Manuel who runs William Morris Endeavor (also famous for being the inspiration for Ari on the HBO series Entourage). From the fashion world they had the group that had invested in Tommy Hilfiger and Michael Kors as well as the family that owns Chanel. Overall, this round was as much about raising influence as it was about raising capital. Having these influencers from key sectors buy into Warby Parker's success was key to get them to the next level. They weren't just looking for checks; they were looking for relationships.

They were really crushing it. Sales were through the roof, and they kept growing. The founders were so overwhelmed with their work that they couldn't meet with investors during normal business hours. But this was such a hot deal that investors were taking the red eye from the West Coast just to sit down for breakfast with the cofounders, so they could get time with them outside of business hours.

In September 2011, Warby Parker raised their second round. This was a $12.5 million round led by Tiger Global—a hedge fund that has been a major investor in Facebook as well as in e-commerce sites like Netshoes (the largest footwear sites in Latin America) and Flipkart (the Amazon.com of India). Their portfolio's companies have had great success partly because they are incredibly thoughtful about how to provide support and expertise. They have experts on retainer to help their investees strategize. The team continued to focus on operational excellence and continued to grow.

In January 2012, Warby raised its third round of $41.5 million, led by General Catalyst Partners. American Express and fashion icon Mickey Drexler, CEO of J Crew, also invested in this round. In the fall of 2013, they raised yet another round of $60 million from the same investors. The fact that the investors keep re-investing in Warby Parker's growth is a sign that the fundamentals of the business are incredibly compelling in this social enterprise.

Warby Parker is a B Corp certified company, a certification for socially and environmentally responsible business. Neil can't remember B Corp certification coming up in the meetings with investors. His sense was that the investors believed that the team knew how to build the brand and if this is part of it, they are fine with it. Most of the investors believed that it was important to invest in good teams, and since they clearly felt Warby Parker was a good team, and the social mission was important to them personally, they were good with it . . . especially since it was making money.

NOT HAVING TO ASK FOR MONEY AGAIN

Many legacy charitable organizations simply raise money from the public without any indication of how that money is going to be used. At times the money has been abused, with almost all of the money going to operations. Charity: Water took the extreme approach to address this problem by creating the 100 percent model; DonorsChoose.org innovated a very smart middle route.

Charles Best was committed to total transparency about where the donor's money was being spent, and he thought it was reasonable to ask donors to support not only specific classroom projects but also to offer some portion of their donation to support the organization. But unlike traditional nonprofits, he wanted to be upfront about this and let donors know that's what would be done. The result was that Charles designed a model that would eventually reach financial sustainability.

When a donor visits a classroom project on the site, they're encouraged, but not required, to allocate 15 percent of their donations to support outreach and overhead costs. The 15 percent is completely optional, but it is the default setting. Donors have to click to choose *not* to donate the 15 percent. Additionally, the 15 percent is included in the amount you want to donate, instead of adding it on. So, say a donor wanted to donate $100 toward a project and wanted to support operations with 15 percent. Her total check out would not be $115, but $100 ($85 going to the classroom project and $15 going to support operations).

This design for checkout is leveraging behavioral economics to achieve an optimal outcome for DonorsChoose.org. First, a surprisingly large number of people in any context tend to stick with the default option, even when it's easy to make changes. Think about the settings on your computer, chances are you've stuck with almost all of the default settings (except for maybe that horrible wallpaper). Second, by including the 15 percent in the total amount the donor is choosing to donate, they are removing a hurdle of adding money to the bill.

A complex checkout process ruins so many transactions in the charitable or the ecommerce world. DonorsChoose.org has kept the checkout process as simple as possible, while still giving the donor choice and transparency. They must be doing something right, because about three quarters of donors keep that 15 percent allocation included. And they have completely funded all operations with that 15 percent since December 2010.

Until DonorsChoose.org broke even, as is common among founders, Charles spent almost half of his time not setting long-term strategy, figuring out how to improve the product, or leading his team, but raising funding for operations. Charles knew he didn't want to do this for the rest of his life. Any founder of a charitable organization knows the feeling. He also knew he wanted the organization to go national. Was there a way to achieve both goals?

The only way to get there was to raise money and scale up rapidly to the point that the money they were raising for operations on the platform actually covered the operational costs. In order to do that, they needed to conduct a significant capital campaign to get them out of the business of fundraising for operations. So, in 2007, that's what they did. Except they did it in a different way than most charitable institutions, they raised it like a tech startup. So, they packed their bags and headed out to Silicon Valley to start pitching.

According to Charles, "We put together a round of funding modeled on a venture capital-style round of funding." They were pitching to the elite Silicon Valley set that had built the dot-com boom in the 1990s and were a new type of philanthropist. Charles framed the conversation the same way that a tech startup would. "We need $14 million to scale up to break even. If we get this infusion of operating capital, we will be able to invest in our organization and grow fast enough that we'll get to scale quickly enough, assuming donors keep that 15 percent allocation included in their donation." Charles said, "We will pay all of our bills before the $14 million runs out."

This was a new spin on philanthropic giving. Instead of milking a high-net-worth donor year after year, they just needed a one-time cash infusion to get to the point that they never needed to raise for operations again. This was appealing to entrepreneurs and venture capitalists that think in those terms every day—identify a web property that has performed well on a small scale, inject cash to fund to scale up, and reach profitability. But rather than the normal financial return on investment, they were going to get a social return on investment.

Charles recalls, "There were varying degrees of excitement around this sort of new approach to funding. I think one or two of those funders had a more classical mindset of this is a great cause. We want to put money behind a great cause that has a great plan for having more impact. Then others in that syndicate were like, this is how the nonprofit sector should apply venture capital startup plans and principles to its work. I'm getting behind this, because I love this idea of participating in a one-time round of funding, and helping an organization hit sustainability, get to breakeven. It was fundamental to those backers that our plan would have us not coming back to them again asking for more money. They were excited that their donation was not creating a dependency. That it was the opposite of creating a dependency."

So, eventually Charles pulled together a syndicate of philanthropists that funded the $14 million from the founder of eBay, co-founder of Yahoo, founder of Netflix, and the founder of Sun Microsystems. They scaled up nationwide and the revenues from check out were eventually enough to bring them to financial sustainability before the $14 million ran out.

"We are completely out of the business of asking people for help with the rent payment, which is very liberating," says Charles. Now the conversation with donors is much more interesting. Rather than appealing to them to help keep the lights on, Charles can have a more interesting discussion with big donors. "It's very different to sit down with them and ask them about their interests and passions and focus their giving directly to the classroom where they can have a direct impact funding something that they are passionate about. 'You like swimming and you like Shakespeare? Well let's talk about a match offer that you could underwrite for swimming and Shakespeare projects on DonorsChoose.org,'" Charles might say. "'Where all of your money would go to these classroom projects.' That's a very different conversation from, 'Please, sir, we need help in keeping our lights on, and paying rent and staff salaries.' The former conversation we still have, the latter conversation we have not had since 2010."

INVESTING IN THE ECOSYSTEM

Most CSR departments at big corporations are there to hedge risk and write a few checks to worthy causes. But Hannah Jones realized the team at Nike should evolve past that. Her vision for where her team could go was much bigger. The story of the pivot she put in motion will be told more fully in a later chapter, but here we'll focus on how the team has implemented a more powerful method for funding causes than the standard corporate approach of simply giving philanthropic funds to organizations.

In 2009, when Nike changed the name of its CSR department to the Sustainable Business and Innovation Lab (SB&I), much more was involved than a name change. The whole emphasis of the group changed from a focus on compliance with high environmental and social responsibility standards to the innovation of more sustainable products. They turned their lens inward on Nike's own product lines (more about that in Chapter 7), but they also decided to begin identifying companies with innovative solutions for driving sustainability to invest in and partner with.

They realized that their goal should be to accelerate innovation and that giving money away wasn't the best way for them to do that. "As we began to think about innovation," Hannah explains, "it became clear that one of the things we were going to have to do was to devise a whole new toolkit." They determined that a key component to accelerating innovation is creating innovation partnerships, which can take many forms, from strategic alliances to joint ventures to investments. So they repurposed some of the team and some of the philanthropic funds and they began hunting for emerging technologies and new startups that could help accelerate, trigger, change, or disrupt materials, products, manufacturing, and services. And they made a substantial commitment to the process, recruiting experts from Venture Capital and Clean Tec. They have invested in a wide variety of companies. One of them is DyCoo, which has disrupted the business of dying textiles by innovating a waterless and chemical-free dying procedure. Typically, the dying process is extremely water intensive. To dye one kilogram of textile requires 115 liters of water. In the apparel industry, this means that every two years they are using the same amount of water that is in the Mediterranean Sea just to dye their clothes. This is a tragic waste, considering the fact that one billion people lack access to clean drinking water globally. Nike loved the company, and it has brought the DyCoo technology into its factories to drastically reduce its water footprint.

Another investment made was in Lavasoft, a software company that works on logistics to help companies lower their carbon footprint from shipping, which was a big issue for Nike itself. Both of these investments have not only supported these innovations, but have helped make improvements to Nike's core business and will help many other companies become more sustainable. That's a great acceleration effect. As Hannah says about the approach "It's both about business and sustainability." Nike's SB&I investment fund will likely yield a substantial financial return for the company in addition to its social return.

KEY TAKEAWAYS

1. Align

Funders invest for a range of reasons. Some are more intent on profits and others on impact. Both can be tough taskmasters. When you are building an organization that is attempting to balance financial return and social and environmental impact, it's important to look for investors who genuinely feel a commitment to your vision. It's also important to such investors that you have an authentic commitment to the purpose you're pursuing. You and your funders must be aligned in your commitments.

Key Question: What funders are committed to the same outcomes I am?

2. Close

After locating funders who are aligned with your mission, you must close the deal by making a persuasive pitch to them, presenting them with clear and easily actionable means to commit funds. Vagueness and shyness are not welcomed by funders. You've got to make a clear ask, including the specific amount of support you're looking for, the timeline you have in mind for the use of the funds, and for the realization of a return if the funds are offered as an investment.

Key Question: What it the appropriate ask for this funder at this time?

CHAPTER FIVE

Connect with Authenticity

All brands today should be rethinking their strategy for reaching consumers, focusing less on traditional advertising and more on the complete customer experience they are offering. The megaphone marketing approach—getting your name in front of consumers and effectively shouting at them about how great you and your products are—has lost its luster. For one thing, consumers are increasingly tuning out on advertising. And, why wouldn't they? So much advertising is gimmicky, shallow, and coercive, and advertisers have generally taken a shotgun approach to reaching consumers, barraging us with poorly targeted ads that are intrusive. Technology now allows us to skip over most ads, either with our DVRs or just by looking away and spending time on our smart phones while they're on.

Meanwhile the Internet has developed into a phenomenally powerful word-of-mouth platform. Gary Vaynerchuck of Vayner Media, a social media agency, argues in his book *The Thank You Economy* that the Web has ushered in a new era of marketing in which consumers are empowered both to seek out more information about brands and to share their experiences with them. Word of mouth can rip around the Web in just moments, and customer reviews speak more loudly than even the most brilliant and best-targeted advertising. Vaynerchuck says that rather than acting like 19-year-old guys trying to close the deal on a first date, brands must work on building lasting relationships with consumers.

Instead of sticking with the megaphone approach, all brands should be taking advantage of new capabilities for drawing customers in, sharing information more openly and honestly, and having authentic, ongoing communication with them. This is the magnet approach to marketing, whether it's creating content that is so compelling that people will actually go out of their way to find it and share it, or offering a more thoughtful shopping experience and higher-quality customer service, or most fundamentally, making products that are more attuned to customers' needs and more in line with their values.

This isn't just a matter of messaging; it's about thinking through every point of contact you have with your customers and making sure you connect with them in a more meaningful and authentic way. As Jeff Rosenblum, the co-founder of innovative advertising agency Questus and director of the documentary *The Naked Brand*, says, "Great experience is not just a big moment, like walking into a retail store or getting on an airplane. It's the moment between the moments. These little granular points of pain that can be turned into points of pleasure." Paying attention to every little moment in your customer's experience of you and your product is a powerful way to build customer loyalty. Like a handwritten thank-you note, it shows you care and it shows you're human.

A clear leader in creating a richer customer experience is Zappos, the online shoe company. Founder and CEO Tony Hsieh believes that providing a truly high-quality customer experience is by far the most effective form of marketing, and the company spends very little on traditional advertising. Instead, Hsieh has focused on offering customers a better experience while buying shoes, such as offering free shipping both ways to ensure customers get the exact right fit and are totally happy with their shoes. For most repeat customers, the company offers an upgrade to free overnight shipping—no small expense. Whereas many retailers hide their phone number deep in the site, Hsieh puts it up front on the homepage and has 24/7 customer support. When a customer calls in they get a person in the United States, who has no script and is committed to staying on the phone as long as necessary to make sure the customer is satisfied. He believes the phone is the best branding device available. In a world where a consumer is constantly bombarded with brand messages, when else do you have the undivided attention of a customer? At Zappos, they see this as an opportunity to forge a real connection with consumers by treating them like human beings and going out of their way to solve their problems. The result for Zappos has been strong customer loyalty and explosive growth.

Patagonia, one of the most successful purpose-driven brands, has been a pioneer of this more authentic and transparent approach to marketing. From the beginning, the brand has made it its mission to produce more environmentally friendly outdoor wear integral to its product development and has communicated about that mission and how it has pursued it to its customers. Recently, the company took a truly courageous step in providing transparency about the environmental impact of its clothing, launching a feature on its web site called the Footprint Chronicles, which offers extensive information about all of the suppliers the company works with and the environmental impact of its use of materials, manufacturing processes, and shipping, making clear that some of those materials and processes are not all that environmentally friendly. They effectively outed themselves for behavior that negatively impacts the environment, but they also communicate through the page about the steps they are making to lessen their environmental footprint. Consumers cheered the initiative because it was honest and showed authenticity of purpose and respect for their concern about the environment. The lesson here is that consumers care more about your value system, intent, and progress toward your goals than they do about perfection.

The message for social enterprises is that they must rethink marketing strategies and work to create innovative campaigns and approaches in their communication with the public that add value to people's lives by connecting through authenticity. A number of the social enterprises profiled in this book have executed this brilliantly.

VALUES DRIVE THE BRAND

Before any brand can have relevant conversation with its consumers, it needs to have a deep understanding of who it is and what it stands for. When ScoJo Foundation rebranded to VisionSpring, they brought in an innovation firm called ?What If!. Neil learned something from this process and used some of those principles when they were launching Warby Parker. The team employed a rigorous method for articulating the brand's values and establishing the order of their priority, which has guided all of their decision making in building the company.

A part of their method involved indentifying the adjectives you believe best describe the nature of the brand and what it stands for; and these words become the building blocks of the brand messaging. Wrestling with the nuances of meaning and associations the words have helps to pinpoint the values that drive you and the character of your brand. For instance, one adjective the founders of Warby Parker agreed described their brand was collegiate, and they chose that word in contrast to preppy. Being collegiate speaks of a desire to better oneself through learning, whereas being preppy suggests a person who comes from privilege and has a vacuous lifestyle, not at all what they wanted their brand to portray.

The team crafted a detailed set of brand values and these have served as a compass for the company, guiding them in all decisions from budgeting to hiring and firing team members. To help the whole team internalize these values and consistently make decisions based on them, they even painted them on the wall of the office kitchen, the most well-trafficked space.

ESTABLISHING THE BRAND HIERARCHY

The branding exercise also establishes a clear brand hierarchy of mission, setting priorities to guide all strategy and marketing.

The team wanted this hierarchy to be in sync with the priorities of their customers and what they value most. So they collected as much data from their target consumers as possible, surveying their friends and classmates. They also went to local optical shops and talked to the salespeople. And once they had samples, they started conducting focus groups. It was a simple setup: Neil would provide the booze and whoever showed up would provide the consumer insights. *In vino veritas*, as the saying goes.

They found that people tended to ask five key questions in considering whether not they would purchase the glasses: "How do these glasses look on my face?," "How much do they cost?," "What are they made of?," and "How did the sales person treat me?" Finally, if it even factored in, "What good does this create?" In accordance with their findings, the brand hierarchy they established is as follows.

Aesthetic

First and foremost, Warby Parker is a fashion brand. Good design is the starting point for any successful fashion brand. So Warby Parker invests in designing frames that look good and are appropriate for their customers. The visual identity, web design, and store layout are all in line with a single aesthetic.

Price

Secondly, the glasses need to be a great value proposition. There is a reason why fast fashion brands like Zara and H&M have become global giants. They have nailed the combination of aesthetics and good pricing. So has Warby Parker.

Customer Experience/Quality

Third and fourth, the glasses need to be high quality, as does the customer service. The customer needs to be able to depend on the glasses to navigate the world day-in and day-out, so they can't break after a couple months. The customer also wants to feel cared for through every interaction that the company has with them, from logging on to trying on to receiving the shipment to calling with questions.

Social Good

Finally, the company should be doing something that matters. This last piece of the brand hierarchy actually did not even register with most people when they were making their purchasing decisions. But, it mattered to the founders, and when the customers knew about the social mission, they appreciated it. The assumption was that from a business standpoint it would help customers enjoy their glasses more. Therefore they would be more loyal and more likely to tell their friends about it.

What's in a Name?

One of the most important aspects of branding is coming up with a name for your organization, and this is one of the hardest features of your brand to change down the road, so it's important to think hard about this.

The Warby team struggled over the name of the company for six months. In the process they came up with 2,000 terrible (Neil's words, not mine) names. Nothing they were coming up with really nailed the essence of the brand they wanted to build. Neil describes how the name was discovered, "One day Dave was wandering around the New York Public Library on 42nd Street when he stumbled into an exhibition about Jack Kerouac. Kerouac had been one of our touchstones throughout the process of defining our brand; we loved the way he inspired a generation to take a road less traveled and see the world through a different lens. The exhibit featured some of Kerouac's manuscripts, notes, drafts, and unpublished journals. Inside one of these journals, Dave noticed two characters with interesting names: Warby Pepper and Zagg Parker. We combined the two and came up with Warby Parker."

For them, the name Warby Parker was a distillation of the essence of who they are. It's memorable, and it has personality, but it also has a deeper meaning. That's the powerful combination you want to shoot for.

GIVE THEM A DELIGHTFUL EXPERIENCE

Another fundamental to the company's branding was crafting an exceptional customer experience. As with Zappos, Warby Parker has distinguished itself by providing a superior shopping experience right from first browsing to customer service.

Anybody who has ever purchased glasses at the optometrist's office or Lens Crafters knows that buying glasses can be overwhelming, confusing, and expensive. The founders knew that no matter how stylish or inexpensive the glasses are, they would not succeed unless they could change the consumer mindset on how they buy glasses.

In order to help the customer choose, they leveraged facial recognition software, which allows the customer to upload a picture and see how the frames would look on his or her face. The customer can browse through the entire catalogue, virtually trying on each pair. After the customer has narrowed down the choices, he or she can choose up to five frames to have shipped to their address as part of the home try-on program, where customers are given a week and encouraged to try them on and see how they look for a while and get the opinion of their friends and family. Recently customers have even been taking pictures of their options and using social media to crowd source their glasses decision. Then they make a selection, upload their prescription information, and the glasses ship out to them. After the customer receives their final pair of glasses, they have 30 days to return, no questions asked. The process is designed to reduce the hassle and anxiety of buying such a personal product online. "We're asking consumers to change the way they buy eyeglasses, so we want to de-risk it as much as possible," says Dave Gilboa.

At any point in the process a customer experience rep is just a phone call away. If you do pick up the phone, you'll notice a few things within the first couple of minutes. First of all, you'll note that you are speaking to a real live American, not an automated system, and not an offshore call center employee. Second you'll notice that they are speaking to you in a conversational tone, not off a script. Lastly you'll notice they are not trying to rush you off the phone. Last year while trying to figure out the logistics of my girlfriend's present, I found myself speaking to a charming woman named Natalie for about 45 minutes.

REWORKING ONE FOR ONE

Integral to the founders' original idea for the company was the plan to distribute one pair of glasses in the developing world for every pair sold. But, unlike other one-for-one models, they don't simply give the pair of glasses away. Instead they partner with VisionSpring to empower entrepreneurs to sell glasses at an affordable cost to those that lack access to glasses. From Neil's experience on the ground he knew that this was a better approach.

But this approach is fairly complex and takes some time to communicate to consumers, so the team struggled with how to promote the program. The challenge was to make the message clear and concise on their web site so consumers would actually make note of it. Neil recalls, "We had so many conversations about what would be on the navigation bar." They ended up listing this under the "Our Story" tab on the home page, and have provided more detail about how the program works through VisionSpring further into the web site, easily clicked on for anyone who wants to probe deeper. They felt this combination allowed them to convey the mission effectively and to offer the transparency that is at the core of their values.

Such decisions about brand messaging can be very difficult to adjudicate, and Neil says the team is still wrestling with this issue and may change the approach at some point. This is just the kind of grappling with how to build an authentic, open, long-term relationship with your customers and the public at large that all social enterprises must engage deeply with.

OFFER DELIGHTFUL EXPERIENCES

One area of brand building in which the company has excelled is in creating promotional experiences that are true to the brand's values.

From the outset, Warby Parker was a scrappy startup that had to be smart with its limited funds and how it chose to spend its marketing dollars. At launch they invested in a PR push to get press in *Vogue* and *GQ*—the top fashion magazines. That worked well to announce the launch of the brand, but after an incredibly successful launch how do you continue to connect with the current customers and grow the customer base?

For its first fashion week presentation in September 2011, they didn't hit the tents of Bryant Park. In a nod to the genesis of their name, Warby Parker took over the reading room at the New York Public Library for a guerilla eyewear show.

The day before the event they sent out invites to fashion editors and fans, which simply read "Meet us at the lions at 3:30." At half-past three, a crowd had assembled by the iconic lions in front of the library. Nobody really knew what was going on. They crowd was led up in pairs to the beautiful main reading room. As they walked in, it looked like business as usual. People were quietly reading their books and milling about.

Vogue describes what happened next, "During a blink-and-you-missed-it event, models and friends of the designers seated around the silent studying room—all wearing Warby Parker shades and glasses—simultaneously raised robin's-egg-blue books, titled with Warby Parker's style names. The collaborative effort provided an interesting and untraditional setting for displaying their spring collection."

The event was technically illegal, done without the permission of the New York Public Library. It was a perfect event for Warby Parker because it was genuine to its brand. First of all, nothing says literary like the main reading room at the New York Public Library, just walking in the room makes you feel more intelligent. This was the exact location where Dave Gilboa came up with the name Warby Parker while viewing an exhibit on Jack Kerouac's unpublished journals. Secondly, it was in the fashion epicenter. All of the big shows were staged at the time in tents at Bryant Park—the lawn directly behind the library. Finally, the guerilla-style move is a nod to the rebellious nature of the company as they are attempting to revolutionize the eyewear industry and wrestle some of the power away from the Luxottica empire. The event was authentic to who they are as a company.

SELECTIVE PARTNERSHIPS

The Standard Hotel is a luxury boutique chain of hotels in New York, Miami, and Los Angeles. The brand is upscale, yet fun and whimsical, a perfect partner for Warby Parker. Their partnership has been long running and together they have produced some unique collaborations, from setting up a small shop in the lobby to sell glasses, complete with an iPad for online ordering, to sponsoring artists-in-residence programs to hosting short story contests.

One effective collaboration happened in the summer of 2013. The Standard New York flies a daily flight from the west side of Manhattan to the Hamptons . . . by seaplane. It's called StndAir. The plane takes off from the Hudson River and flies east to the Hamptons. Every passenger on StndAir was provided with a pair of Warby Parker shades and a Cliffs Notes-style version of a classic piece of literature, since the ride is fairly quick.

Warby Parker has formed a number of other effective partnerships. In addition to their normal giving for eyewear through Vision-Spring, occasionally the company will create a limited-edition frame featuring a specific nonprofit partner. Each nonprofit collaboration takes one of the company's popular frames and gives them a little twist—usually a splash of color identified with that nonprofit. This technique allows them to create a product that they know consumers already like, but with a splash of individuality for the customer to tell the story of their support. They have collaborated with Invisible Children, to help eradicate the Lord's Resistance Army (LRA) in Northern Uganda and the Democratic Republic of Congo; with Susan G. Comen Foundation to fight breast cancer; with Pencils of Promise to help build schools in the developing world; and with DonorsChoose.org to help fund classroom projects. In the summer of 2013, they did a mass-market partnership with the summer blockbuster Superman film *Man of Steel*, in which they encourage Superman fans to "empower the next generation" through the purchase of the frames—strikingly similar to Clark Kent's signature frames. For every pair they sell, Warby Parker will donate $15 to 826NYC to help students increase their writing skills.

HIT THE ROAD JACK

Being an online brand has its advantages—operational costs, automation, supply chain to name a few—but no matter how great you are at creating a connection with your customer online, that relationship still lacks a personal feel that comes with face-to-face encounters. Again calling on the inspiration of the brand's literary hero Jack Kerouac, they decided to hit the road and bring the brand to the people. So they bought a classic yellow school bus, ripped out the old green vinyl seats, and proceeded to build out an interior that aligned with the brand inspired by old libraries, professor's offices, mid-century modern design, and vintage Rolls Royce interiors. The result, after a four-month build out, was a mobile show room kitted out with oak shelves, a chalkboard, a distinguished library, and the entire selection of Warby Parker optical and sunglasses.

The custom school bus was staffed with enthusiastic, road-ready Warby Parker employees, and they headed west from New York, hitting the major cities across the United States. They pull into a city, co-host a couple of events at local retailers, park the bus, and open up the bus for business. The customers can browse, try on, and order their frames from the bus via iPad. Or they can just plop down on the couch and read one of the books in the library.

THE MARKETING METHOD TO THE MADNESS

Method doesn't have a marketing team. They have a brand experience team. That's because they don't see marketing as distinct from the rest of their design process.

Marketing for the company is about influencing customers and potential customers' decision-making behavior. This was a bold decision for the company, but the founders didn't believe they could compete in advertising in the cleaning products world. The marketing budgets of their competitors are equivalent to the GDP of some small nations. So, in their scrappy style, they decided to go against the conventional wisdom and skip the big marketing budget in an effort to create a brand that was more human and interesting.

Method starts by trying to understand the consumer's motivations. Why do they buy a product? They think of customer desires as structured similarly to Maslow's famous hierarchy; the bottom of the pyramid are the actual needs of the consumer—in this case effective products for cleaning the house—and at the top of the pyramid are the wants of the consumer—his or her aspirations. When you are just competing on the needs of the consumer, a race to the bottom occurs and the brand becomes about a list of features and price competition. The product is simply a commodity. So Method focuses on raising the consumer's decision making up the pyramid toward their wants and aspirations.

In order to encourage this journey, Method focuses on creating a great brand experience. "What's a better experience? It's one that's memorable, remarkable, or unexpected in some way." According to Adam and Eric, "It's what keeps people coming back to you instead of your competitors. Like it or not, a quality product just isn't enough. Today, quality is only the price of entry. Products fulfill needs. *Experiences fulfill desires.*" We are drowning in a sea of goods, with more choices of products than any other time in history. Most of the needs of Method's target consumers have been satisfied, so the company wants to compete on emotional sensibility. In a society where most needs are met, experiences become more important. Of course a good product matters, but they needed to deliver on something the competition couldn't. Method set out to change the experience of cleaning, to make cleaning fun.

The law of supply and demand dictates that a consumer will pay a premium for something that is scarce. In the world of cleaning, nothing is more scarce than fun. Repositioning the purchase of a cleaning product from simply a rational decision to an emotional decision is the crux of Method's obsession with product experience. Whereas marketing is usually thought about after the product is designed, with Method brand experience is integrated into the design process from the beginning. Method builds marketing into the product itself.

Most design processes start with a design brief describing the criteria that the product needs to meet. At Method, the brand is the brief. It's the starting point for all of the products they make. The basis for a product that creates a great experience is having a clear understanding of the brand, then thinking about how that extends into the product experience.

The best brands have a clearly articulated point of view (POV) that is distinctive and uniquely their own. Method's POV is inclusive, optimistic, simple, and aspirational—or, to take it directly from their brand DNA statement, "smart, sexy, and sustainable." At Method the brand experience doesn't begin with getting "inspiration" (aka copying) other brands, but looking internally at who they are and starting to build out from there.

Smart, sexy, and sustainable are great, but how does that translate into an actual product you can use? Most companies have brand pillars; Method uses experience pillars. The experience pillars are the formula that needs to be perfect before a product is released. The experience pillars give direction to design, but also help edit the product and tell Method what not to do. The pillars keep the designers accountable to the brand experience. This approach has two main benefits: the consumer gets a better experience and Method gets a competitive advantage. Additionally, the pillars are scaleable. If you design a good product, you have one good product, but if you build pillars, you have a platform for an infinite number of products based on those pillars.

Adam and Eric describe how the brand pillars guided their baby line, "As the company was growing up, we all started having babies, so when we couldn't find baby products with a strong sense of individual design and a belief in greener solutions, we decided to create them ourselves. Conscientious parents love the mild ingredients—like rice milk and mallow—and they applaud the lack of harmful chemicals, like phthalates and parabens (which major baby brands had been hiding off-label for years). But it wasn't ingredients alone that helped our baby line stand out. Keeping in line with our obsessions, the cartoony bottles were eye-catching and made from sustainable materials. And the line was designed with the real-world experiences of busy, preoccupied parents in mind. Our diaper cream features a one-handed pump for no-mess usage and our baby wash includes an oversize cap that doubles as a rinsing cup. As stand-alone features, each was a minor triumph in industrial design; collectively, the line exemplifies the dynamic power of Method's obsession with product experience." Product experience is about being refreshing to consumers.

At Method, "cutting steel" is a marketing expense, or more specifically, it's an investment in brand experience. In order to make a custom product, a company first has to build a mold, which starts out as a big block of steel that is then cut into the shape of the product. In the industry, this is known as cutting steel, and it's an exacting and expensive process. For Method the commitment to cutting steel for one bottle is about $150,000. Many companies forgo this expensive process and just go with a stock bottle that the manufacturer has on hand—thus the proliferation of unoriginal bottles on the shelf at your local store.

For most of Method's competitors, the ROI on cutting steel doesn't make sense, they would rather spend their money in marketing the product. Method sees this issue in reverse. When they compared the cost of creating a unique bottle and the cost of marketing, they found that investing in creating a unique bottle is a relative bargain. That $150,000 invested in a mass-marketing campaign would not even buy a quarter page ad in a national magazine. Conversely, the bottle has generated millions in free press and buzz as well as getting the attention of retailers and driving sales on the shelf. "Our belief was that if we created a product that exceeded expectations, people would talk about it and drive word of mouth." Adam and Eric say "Because Method could never win the advertising battle by shouting louder, we needed the product to shout for us. We believe you should go into any product development process with the assumption there will be no marketing support and that the product needs to be special and differentiated enough to stand on its own. Marketing should be rocket fuel to propel a great product, not the Hail Mary for a mediocre product." Cutting steel is one way that Method focuses on creating a great experience.

Rationality will put you in the running, but it won't win the race. In a crowded marketplace, you can count on the fact that just about every one of your competitors will meet the standard of rationality. Method makes a product that works, it is a rational choice for the consumer, but in order to close the sale it focuses on creating an emotional experience for the consumer. Building that emotional connection has positive short-term benefits in the form of the immediate sale, and long-term benefits in the form of greater customer loyalty than brands that don't connect emotionally with the consumer.

Delivering on emotional experiences means engaging the senses, the fast track to human emotion. To the team at Method, that visceral negative reaction of the senses seemed quite unclean. So, they created a new sensory experience with a clean design that appeals to our aesthetic sense, formulas that actually feel clean, and fragrances that smell great. Additionally, they focused on the sense of touch in their experience by creating packaging that is organically and ergonomically shaped and invites touch. The result is a full sensory experience—smell, touch, sight—that can make the dreaded task of cleaning a bit more pleasant. Adam and Eric describe it this way, "We build emotional points of difference into every product to create an engaging consumer experience. We do this by dramatically challenging existing alternatives on every front, from the use of unexpected fragrances like sea minerals to packaging copy that talks about angry squirrels. Great experiences are about being human, and humans want to be surprised. Basic categories like soap offer few opportunities for differentiation, so you have to sweat the details. The way the label feels in your hand, the shape of the bottle on your counter, the sound of the trigger being squeezed, the writing on the back of a bottle that makes you chuckle, even the little surprise of an owner's manual inside a candle box."

But, a word of caution, great experiences are polarizing. Since an experience is inherently subjective and dependent on personal taste, don't expect everybody to love what you are doing. Method believes that it's better to alienate 90 percent of consumers in favor of making a deep connection with 10 percent. The alternative, which is a death knell for any brand, is just being okay for everybody. Adam and Eric think of it in this way, "The result: fewer customers (less market share) buying more of your stuff (more wallet share). The idea of flipping the pyramid scares a lot of business leaders because it means focusing on a smaller audience. But in a world with less effective forms of mass media, you have no choice but to focus on a narrower audience to build an efficient marketing model."

Method also engages in ongoing communication with customers. The founders understand that they are not in control of the conversation online, but they do their best to be receptive, in every medium, from old-fashioned snail mail and the phone to tweeting and blogging. They even give their email addresses out so you can reach out to them directly at the end of their book (but you'll have to buy it first!).

They believe by listening to the conversation they can learn a great deal about the product, how it's actually being used, and what type of experiences they are creating. Method started out by listening. At their very first store in 2002, Adam and Eric were in the stores getting customer feedback. Back then the customer service line rang directly to their cell phones. The habit of listening was ingrained from day one, and in order to stay great listeners they in-source customer service, advocacy communications, PR, design, and creative. Beyond listening to, and taking the feedback from customers seriously, Method is committed to creating advocates. They have engaged with their consumers to help them spread the word.

Take Nathan Aaron, for instance. Nathan really likes Method . . . I mean *really* likes it. So much so that he started a blog called methodlust.com. Yes, apparently Method does have a fan club and Nathan is the president. Methodlust.com features products, gives reviews, talks about rumored new products in the pipeline, has exclusive interviews with more than 30 of the Method staff, and even shows alternative uses for Method products like using the shower spray as a bug repellant and using old bottles for lamp shades. Nathan started this site and built a loyal audience on his own, but Method was happy to help out in any way it could, like supplying information to him first or getting him interviews and product photos, and so on.

Nathan not only sings Method's praises, he also keeps them accountable by giving negative reviews and feedback from his followers. A helpful ally and, occasionally, a loving adversary, Nathan represents the ideal brand advocate.

Method also likes to look for opportunities to call its fans and advocates into action. One day a letter arrived in the mail from the Clorox company filled with threatening legal jargon. The letter basically demanded that Method cease and desist from using the daisy in their ads (which they had been doing from the very early stages to show that the products were so natural they wouldn't hurt a daisy). Clorox claimed that they owned the trademark on the daisy for their new line of green cleaning products (not one of their finer moments). Adam recalls, "Some poor lawyer forgot to check his history. And he sent us a cease and desist letter that had all of this language like: Clorox has invested millions to associate its brand with the environment. We are a leader in a green cleaning category, and all this stuff in their letter, and threatening to sue us."

What seemed at first as an aggravating or potentially very harmful legal problem, Method turned into an opportunity to engage their fans and advocates. A part of Method's ethos had always been that they were a challenger brand, a rebel with a cause disrupting the status quo. So, they decided this was a perfect moment. Instead of fighting a legal battle with a huge corporation employing a phalanx of lawyers, they decided to take it to the court of public opinion.

So they sent a letter to Clorox saying, "Isn't it silly for us to fight over a flower? Why don't we let the people decide who should own the daisy?" They invited the public to cast their vote at votedaisy.com, a micro site where they posted Clorox's cease-and-desist letter alongside a video of Adam and Eric explaining the situation, and an invitation to vote on who should own the daisy— Method, Clorox, or Mother Earth. Adam and Eric said, "Within hours of launch, votedaisy.com was picked up by the *New York Times*. Thousands of people voted, and naturally, Mother Earth won by a landslide. And in a testament to advocate loyalty, hundreds of lawyers sent us free legal advice, assuring us that we were in the right. Suffice it to say, we never heard back from Clorox."

"The difference between a mass-market brand and a belief brand is like the difference between a monologue and a dialogue," according to Adam and Eric. "Mass brands talk at people. Or more accurately, they SHOUT! Belief brands, on the other hand, listen and create a conversation." The belief brands don't offer a promise; they help you live better. That message is more nuanced and complex than a simple jingle will allow. So, they invite the consumer into a deeper and richer relationship.

Belief brands were at a disadvantage in the mass media age. But in the social media age, they are in an advantageous position for two reasons. First, the belief brand can have a richer dialogue, but, perhaps more importantly, the transparency that social media brings can call out promise brands on their shallowness and their inability to deliver on their promises.

As the next generation comes to own more and more of the purchasing power, mass media brands are going to increasingly lose their competitive advantage, undermined by a desire for connection with a brand based on shared values.

DON'T TALK AT YOUR CUSTOMERS, LISTEN TO THEM

Soma's Kickstarter campaign didn't just bring in $150,000 to the company, it also gave them vital information to help with their product launch. They had just more than 2,300 backers on Kickstarter, but Soma saw these 2,300 people as a huge opportunity to understand their community.

They sent out a survey via email to those Kickstarter backers. Out of 2,300 backers, they had nearly 900 responses to a 17-question survey. This is an incredibly high level of engagement. Typical response rates for surveys are below 10 percent. So getting 900 respondents to the survey is huge.

One of the questions on the survey was "Would you be open to a short phone call so we could learn more about you?" Three hundred people said yes. So they hired a consultant to go through all of that data and make phone calls. They ended up speaking to 50 to 100 people. Through these surveys and calls they got to know their core customer pretty intimately, gaining a clearer understanding of what experiences and frustrations users had with the existing water filters. Perhaps more importantly, they figured out why their core audience would be persuaded to purchase a Soma filter. It turns out that they would purchase first for the design, then for the contribution to sustainability, and thirdly for the ease of the subscription model for replacement filters. The fact that the product was made in America was a close fourth.

The research also revealed their users' reading preferences, which helped them target their marketing. Two of the favorite blogs were Fast Company and Dwell. So, they knew that collaboration with those outlets was important. They also captured basic demographic information. Based on all of this information, they started building customer archetypes, creating four of them. One was "The Techie." The Techie is a fab.com buyer. He/she lives in an urban environment, is 25 to 35 years old, single and very tech savvy (maybe an engineer or a designer), very active on social media, and takes pride in being on the leading edge. They want to know what's cool and hot. They really magazines like *Fast Company* and blogs like Reddit, Thought Catalog, or Cool Hunting.

"We literally had photos on our wall of these archetypes," Mike says. "That really helped us to hone in our marketing strategy for the official launch."

BUILDING A COMMUNITY

Armed with this information about their customers, Soma began to build their strategies. The first key strategy for the product launch was to engage their community. They already had a solid community of backers from Kickstarter, but they wanted to extend that community to include influencers and editors.

Mike thought the best way to get people excited about the product was for them to experience it first hand in its natural setting. So, they decided to host a few exclusive underground dinner parties. One such event they co-hosted with *Dwell* magazine in an impeccably designed house in Venice, California. They did another in New York City with editors from major publications like the *New York Times* and *Vogue*. They hosted still other events with the Silicon Valley crowd in San Francisco.

The parties are intimate, only 20 people each time. Guests are not allowed to talk about it, no social media is permitted, and the secret location is revealed the day of the event. The point of the dinner is to invite influencers into the Soma community, and to give them a sense of the product without saying much about it. Mike didn't want this to be too much about the product, but more about the experience and the community. Mike says, "We don't really tell them much about Soma. We just treat them to a really wonderful night that involves community story telling. We show a Charity: Water video. So they get our commitment to giving back and sustainability. They get to drink the water from Soma. They see how beautiful it is on the table. They meet all the other people who are passionate about Soma."

PRESS COVERAGE TRUMPS ADS

The second key to connecting with their audience prior to launch was lining up media. Mike says, "One of the things that I say is that a product launch you have to win the battle before it begins. So we hustled to lock in a lot of press." Their hustle paid off, because they had more than 40 stories confirmed prior to launch.

Unlike the promotion for the Kickstarter campaign, for the product launch nine months later, they split the media work between their team and a PR agency. They were aware that in order to get the top-tier publications that they didn't have relationships with, they were going to need some outside help.

Prior to the Kickstarter campaign, Mike was introduced to Ben Goldhirsh the founder of *GOOD*. Ben said, "We are really focused on building a community. We have the magazine, but it is really about this online community and democratizing the conversation. Why don't you just get involved? Start posting on good.is, and favoriting people, following them and just getting involved in general in the community."

So Mike started doing that, and when it came time to launch the Kickstarter campaign, he just wrote one blog post on Soma. Why Soma started it, why it is important, and why it is relevant to the GOOD community. That post ended up going into an email that was sent to all the email subscribers and it ended up being the driver of the traffic, with the most people actually buying the water filter.

So, when they were preparing for their product launch in September, Mike went back to Ben and said, "Hey, by a very large margin GOOD was the biggest driver of sales for Kickstarter. I think that's really cool and I just wanted to celebrate that with the GOOD community, and tell them that story. Then also highlight the fact that we are officially launching. So that if you didn't back our Kickstarter you could actually buy the product."

That letter to the GOOD community was emailed out to every-one, and it was the top driver of sales, outperforming sites with

10 times their traffic. For Soma, GOOD was a perfect fit for their savvy, sustainable audience.

BUILD MOMENTUM WITH A PRE-LAUNCH CAMPAIGN

The week before the product launch, Soma conducted a pre-launch campaign.

From the time the Kickstarter ended until the week before Soma launched, the web site was a single page that had a photo of the filter and read, "Soma the smart beautiful sustainable water filter. Sign up to be the first to know when we launch." The page was just there to collect emails.

The week before launch they turned that page dark—from white to black. There was a mysterious image of the Soma carafe and a countdown to launch. The text read "Get early access to the limited first round", creating an air of mystery and allure, which allowed them to collect a great deal of emails.

On launch day, they turned on a beautiful bright, shiny, white site. They turned the lights back on and made Soma available for purchase for the first time. Mike says, "That sequence of building up into a spatial loop was really important. It was a key part of the overall campaign."

The strategy paid off. Their traffic was through the roof and they blew away their sales expectations. But this was only the starting point for Soma. As soon as they celebrated a great launch, they had to turn their focus toward their first holiday season.

Amidst the endless sea of products competing for our attention, how could they get Soma water filters under the Christmas tree?

To that end, they were selected to be part of an exhibit called Divine Details with 40 of the most well-designed products of the year that ran in November and December 2013. The goal of the gallery is to change the way American consumers think about shopping—shifting a mindset from quantity to quality.

Divine Details was curated by the New York City design duo Tina Chang and Esther Mun, known as Little Fury. When visitors walk into the gallery, there is a coat check and 40 items displayed as pieces of art. Each item has a description from a professional writer.

If you like an item you can purchase it, but it's a totally different experience than a normal retail store that is organized into aisles with 200 items stacked on a shelf. There are no carts or baskets, nothing to get in the way of the consumer connecting with the story of each item.

Mike says, "The whole point of the exhibit is to ask consumers, why do you look at products different than we would look at a work of art? Why don't we select pieces that you want to own for the rest of your life, and be very careful about what your purchase? And really think about everything that goes into it, the sustainability, is there a charitable aspect? How is it going to impact your life? How is it going to impact the environment? We love that, that is so Soma."

There are competing views on how to create the best product and tell the best story for consumers. On the one hand, you have the Steve Jobs perspective. Jobs is famous for leading Apple to launch breakthrough products that none of us could have imagined were possible. I remember the first time I saw an iPhone, I was blown away that a phone could allow me to surf the Web, schedule meetings, and check email, and that it could do it in such an elegant design. When I first laid hands on one (it was a late night dinner with friends in Manhattan), I went straight to the Apple store at 2:00 a.m. and bought one.

From Jobs's perspective, truly meaningful, delightful, and game-changing products—products that make somebody need to run to the store in the middle of the night to purchase one—are products that the customer has never conceived of. He thought it was his job as a salesperson to tell the customer what they want. Jobs is famous for quoting Henry Ford, "If I asked the customer what they wanted, they would have said a faster horse."

On the other hand, you have the Lean Startup methodology, which is all about gaining constant customer feedback and continually tweaking your product to align with what the customer wants. This approach gives product designers rapid feedback and allows them to continually iterate toward a product that meets the needs of the consumer. Indeed, the whole process of product design is seen as an experiment to understand the consumer better.

Soma tries to take the best from both approaches. According to Mike, "I think with Soma we are on both sides of the equations. On one hand we have a very strong point of view. It starts with design and it incorporates sustainability. When we design our products we design an entire experience, so we want to make your life easier with the subscription. The heart of the organization is giving. So we wouldn't want to create a product that just benefits our customers; it must also benefit those most in need. That happens to be our brand hierarchy. Thankfully when we did customer research, we found out that that is exactly what the customers wanted as well. First, they wanted strong design, but their second priority was that the product contributes to sustainability.

Soma has created what seems to be a strong and growing niche by engaging its audience with a well-designed product that also happens to be made from sustainable materials and supports a social program. They are also constantly cultivating their community.

KEY TAKEAWAYS

There are two key ways to make your outreach to consumers convey authenticity and to build a strong, long-term connection.

1. Experience over Advertising

Authenticity begins with integrity. When actions line up with the values, the social enterprise has earned the right to be heard. Actions speak louder than words. Social entrepreneurs must tell a compelling story with their actions; more than anything, that will create an authentic connection with consumers. Customers understand that a brand cares about them when they have intentionally designed a meaningful experience.

The return on investment for this extra effort and expense is customer delight, and delight yields not only loyalty but brand evangelists who will spread your message much more powerfully than any amount of advertising could.

Authenticity is how the customer is treated at every stage of the customer experience. A brand is built by every touch point it has with the customer—from first hearing about the product through and after the purchase. Creating a meaningful experience takes a great deal of discipline and intention.

The experience from start to finish communicates to the customer that you care about taking the hassle out of their lives and giving them some boost of enjoyment and satisfaction.

Key Question: Where are the opportunities for me to delight my customers in our interaction?

2. Honesty over Perfection

For-purpose organizations, by definition, are holding themselves to a higher standard, which should be honored and respected. Those social/environmental standards should never be watered down or compromised. In fact, the for-purpose organization should continually strive to improve. But that doesn't mean they need to be perfect.

Alex Bogusky, named "Creative Director of the Decade" by *AdWeek,* notes that consumers can be quite understanding. "As long as they know that you're trying, they will forgive you. There is no human being in this world that's perfect. Corporations are just an organism; they are a collection of individuals, so none of them are perfect."

The level of transparency is only increasing. Apps are entering the market that allow consumers to see right though the packaging and the marketing and all that brand speak and figure out is it the appropriate product for them based on their values. In this world of increasing transparency, it's essential that social enterprises lead the way in being honest, not perfect.

Key Question: Where do I need to be honest with my consumers about our shortcomings?

CHAPTER SIX

Scale Through Community

You've launched and the market is responding well. Your product or service is hot, and the press and user reviews are good. Your revenue and user base is strong, and the opportunities for growth seem bountiful. This period after a successful launch can be enormously exciting and satisfying. But as the founders of even the most successful organizations learn, the opportunities for failure are also bountiful. And the tricky issues in balancing the pursuit of purpose and profit can make managing growth even more difficult.

How does a social enterprise grow intelligently? How does it scale up without losing sight of its purpose or its leadership getting stretched too thin? The answer is through community building, both inside the organization and in the community at large.

As an organization grows from a scrappy little startup with a team of 5 or maybe 20 in one office, to a team of 100 or more often scattered across several offices and around the country, the spirit of mission and the alignment around what the organization stands for shared by the tight-knit initial team can be lost in the frenzy of managing organizational issues. Dealing with the basic business or organizational challenges, whether staffing, sales and marketing, inventory control, and IT systems, can suck the energy out of founders and their management teams. As people's jobs become more specialized, they become siloed into departments or teams, and there is less understanding around the organization about issues being faced and about the factors in management decisions. At the same time, bringing in so many new people can have a transformative effect on the organization's culture, the tone of the work environment, the ethic about how colleagues treat one another, and the nature of communication with customers—all of those little touch points within and without an organization that constitute its culture—become harder for founders to control.

This means that growth requires a more intentional nurturing of culture and a concerted, self-conscious effort to keep the entire team focused on the values of the organization and its purpose. The founders of the organizations profiled in this book have developed or adopted a number of great methods for doing so.

MAKING A MISSION TRULY MEANINGFUL

At the time that Rob Kalin was formulating his idea for Etsy, he was heavily influenced by reading two books: *Deep Economy*, which is about creating local economies, and *Small Is Beautiful*, which articulates the struggle between economic growth and the human cost of globalization. When the company was a scrappy 15-employee operation, eveyone was given a copy of *Deep Economy*, and there were many copies of *Small is Beautiful* floating around the office. The founders wanted Etsy to be a company that stood for the values those books espoused, and Rob wrote a founding mission statement: "Etsy swings the pendulum back to a time when we bought our shoes from the cobbler, bread from the baker." The focus was on reconnecting people, and bringing humanity into commerce. But as the company rapidly grew, its culture drifted from the spirit of those early days.

The pressing day-to-day concerns of running a growing startup took precedence, and the founder's focus turned to issues like retaining the right employees, firing the right employees, putting financial procedures in place, and warding off lawsuits. As the company kept growing, it was able to attract star talent, and the founders hired experts away from Google and other high-powered companies to help them scale up. But while this injection of professionalism helped bring the chaos of growth into good working order and set the company up for long-term success, the core values were being eclipsed.

Growth continued apace, and in 2007, Rob took on the job of launching a European headquarters in Berlin. He had a high level of autonomy there, and he started to focus again on the social and environmental mission. At fashion week in 2009, he ran a campaign called *Fashion Does Not Equal Industry*. "We wanted to talk about some of the ecological and social consequences of fast fashion," he recalls. Fast fashion has created a highly disposable wardrobe devoid of connection and meaning.

Not long after, Rob and his wife had a child, which inspired him to start thinking more about the long-term environmental impact of the business and how problems like climate change would affect his child's life. In both 2009 and 2010, he attended the World Economic Forum and learned from business leaders around the world about the approaches being taken to address the panoply of pressing global issues. He also began to practice Buddhist meditation and learning about Buddhism, which emphasizes the interconnectivity of all living beings. One of the principles of the eightfold path of Buddhism is right livelihood, and Rob felt inspired by that to commit to making a more substantial social and environmental impact through his work.

Rob decided that it was either time for him to move on from Etsy or to push for the company to become more socially and environmentally concerned. A couple of years later Rob returned to Brooklyn. At that point, he started to formalize a revised mission statement for the company. The original one had not been aspirational or really inspirational enough, he'd decided. He and his team drafted a Manifesto of Responsibility. They took inspiration from a famous Buckminster Fuller quote: "You never change things by fighting the existing reality. To change something, build a new model that makes the existing model obsolete." Grass roots activist campaigns like Move Your Money Day also inspired them. People just walked into their banks and took their money out to express their opposition to the banks' ethics and values, and in one day they moved $4 billion. That was a powerful statement.

To further the commitment to the values the management team decided to to ahead with an idea that Matt Stinchcomb and Rob Kalin had talked about for some years and establish the company as a B Corp. In the process of pursuing certification, they learned that the company barely passed the minimum standards for environmental certification. They got the certification, but they also decided that was just the beginning. They realized they had to engage all the employees in order to create a culture in support of the missions, so they held a B Corp Hack Day.

The entire office was shut down for a day, and the whole staff focused on developing strategies for increasing the company's social and environmental performance. They decided to use the measures of the B Corp scoring system to guide them, which they knew would also provide clear metrics for measuring their progress.

The employees were split up into teams and each was tasked with putting forward a proposal. The team determined to have come up with the most practical idea that would have the most impact on the score would win a prize.

The ideas that came out of the Hack Day resulted in many initiatives: tracking the company's whole ecological footprint, offering day care, creating a volunteer platform, and instituting programs to encourage women to take on more leadership roles in the company. But the founders say that the biggest institutional impact of that Hack day was the successful refocusing of the whole staff on the newly articulated mission. They have also created a core group of employees who are tasked with maintaining that focus and continuing to implement initiatives toward the social and environmental responsibility goals, which were made part of the standards evaluating employees in their annual performance reviews.

The Etsy founders were able to recognize the company's cultural drift and to use simple methods for generating a new clarity of mission and company-wide commitment to it. Another company that has used a simple tool to assure that a growing staff is aligned around its mission is Warby Parker.

KEEPING ON TOP OF EMPLOYEE ENGAGEMENT

Neil Blumenthal was the captain of his basketball team in high school. Born and bred in New York City, he's a Knicks fan, strongly resisting the Nets bandwagon preferred by his hipster customers in

Brooklyn. Growing up playing on sports teams, it's not surprising that his management philosophy has been shaped by his experience.

Neil sees the employees of Warby Parker as a team, not a family as many companies claim. Neil explains why the distinction is important, "The difference being that on a sports team everybody has signed up and volunteered to participate in something because they believe in the mission and accomplishing something great. Nobody gets to choose their family, we're all born into it. Most of the time that's great, but when the crazy drunk uncle embarrasses the family at a Thanksgiving, he's still part of the family whether you like it or not. Conversely, people are invited to join a team and voluntarily accept the invitation. So the team member shows aptitude and promise prior to joining the team and they want to be there. Also, when the team is really united on achieving a great goal they are going to keep each other accountable. If one team member is not pulling their weight, they are going to hear it from their teammates and the coach is going to bench you. In this way the team, and more importantly, the team's goals take precedence over the individual . . . even the stars of the team."

As a coach of the team, Neil has had to grow in his leadership ability. He admits that he naturally prefers to be liked rather than being respected. But he knows that to be an effective coach he has to be respected. A big part of that is honesty and accountability. So, Neil knew he needed to put some practices in place.

The team has grown incredibly rapidly, from 100 employees to 175 during 2012 and to 250 in 2014. In managing this growth, the founders have made use of a very effective basic tool, a weekly 5-15 report.

They took the idea from Patagonia founder Yvon Chouinard. The concept is that every week, every employee writes what he or she accomplished during the week and at the same time writes a plan for next week. The secret to the 5-15 report is in its brevity. It should take no longer than 15 minutes to write and 5 minutes to read. The intent is two-fold: to celebrate what you've accomplished and prepare and plan for next week, so that you can accomplish more.

Neil and his team have "Warby-ized" (his phrase, not mine) the 5-15 a bit by adding two additional pieces of information.

Employees are asked to suggest an idea for innovation. This can be a huge innovation or a small tweak, they just have to suggest something. One such idea concerned the break room. It was incredibly simple, but it has had a great effect. An employee noted that there were often bottlenecks to get to the sink in the company kitchen because so many people were filling up their water bottles at it, and she suggested placing a water cooler outside the room. The management team loved the idea and implemented it immediately. This is not an idea that will change the course of the company, but such responsiveness to employees signals to them that their ideas matter, even the small ones, and that Warby Parker is a place that values ideas. Also, as a part of the 5-15 report employees are asked to rate their happiness on a scale of 1 to 10. The goal is to closely monitor employee satisfaction, and this simple procedure helps managers understand when people are getting unhappy and to initiate a conversation to help turn things around. Again, it also sends a strong message that the management cares about how employees are feeling.

The 5-15 report is just a tool. Like any other tool, it can be used effectively or ineffectively. In order for the 5-15 reports to be effective, the managers need to be engaged in the process and take it seriously. The two keys to effective use of the 5-15 report are immediate feedback and connection to the larger vision of the company.

Immediate feedback is provided to the employee the next working day. The point of this is to make sure that the employee understands that this report is not just going into the ether, but that his manager is on top of his progress and that she has listened and considered the employee's ideas. The manager will tell the employee immediately whether his idea is going to be implemented or not, assuring every employee knows listening is truly a priority.

Another benefit of the 5-15 report is that it operates as a weekly check on how each individual and each team is progressing toward the annual goals of the company. Neil notes that, "if the 5-15 reports are done well, they're just weekly analytics on how we're incrementally moving toward our goals. I like that." These reports help managers understand how to effectively set priorities among their team and whether they need to shift priorities to achieve the overall company goals.

WILD GROWTH

Going national with Target led to phenomenal growth for Method, of about 200 percent per year. By 2006 Method was the seventh fastest growing company in the United States, and in an industry that had been in decline. They hit $100 million in revenue in less than eight years.

As they grew rapidly, the big boys in the industry began to take notice. Apparently green cleaning products sell well, so they started making their own. It was at this point that the founders of Method truly understood the multiplying effect of their mission and saw the true power of business as a social-change agent. Rather than viewing the competition as knocking their ideas off, Method sees itself as a company that innovates, proves the concept, and eventually the bigger brands slowly see that it works and start to do the same. The upside of this is that the mission of bringing natural products and high design to consumers is being multiplied. So, by proving that there is a market for products with purpose, they have changed the practices of a whole industry. They proved that purpose can drive profit.

As they grew, they extended the brand in many ways. They started a show on HSN (the Home Shopping Network), launched an automotive brand called Vroom, launched an air care brand—taking them into electronics, and created a body-care line. Adam and Eric recall, "This wasn't your typical start-up growth; this was wild, uninhibited growth—the kind that affords all sorts of insights along the way and the kind that—at least temporarily—hides all your sins and bad habits."

Brand extension is one of the most difficult aspects of growth, for organizations of all kinds. Even giant corporations often get it wrong. Just think about New Coke, or more recently the Facebook phone. Deciding to create a new product line, or to expand your service to additional areas must be done carefully, with a thorough assessment of how the new initiative fits into your overall strategy and aligns with your mission. For social enterprises, the pressure to expand comes not only from the business mandate to always keep growing, but also from the sense of mission. If a program is helping underprivileged youth in one city, shouldn't you bring it to as many others as possible? If your products are keeping toxic chemicals out of people's homes and out of landfills and the watershed, shouldn't you keep making more of them? But without the right analysis and rollout process, even brand extensions that seem obvious and like sure bets can trip you up.

In all of the frenzy of Method's rapid growth, a big new product that seemed to have everything going for it was a stark lesson in taking carefully measured steps and doing lots of market research and testing. Adam and Eric had been eyeing the personal-care category for a while. From the beginning customers had been sending letters asking them to make a personal-care line, and it seemed like a logical move. They were already making hand soap, so why not just fully commit to the category?

But they knew they had to bring something unique to the category. Unlike home care, many personal care brands had been using high design in their products for some time, so every imaginable shape of bottle was already on the shelves. If Method was going to bring its concept of unique design to the personal-care shelf, they'd need to do something more. They came up with square bottles that fit together like Legos and had a texture similar to that of a bar of soap, which they named the Bloq line.

Despite the great packaging, Bloq failed for a number of fundamental reasons. First, they had let the business drive the brand, rather than the brand driving the business. They jumped in because of the attractive margins, but they lacked the unique perspective on body care that they had for home care. Also, in the home care line, they had capitalized on a major cultural shift, leading the way in a new category. But body care had moved into natural products many years earlier.

They also failed to conduct proper market testing, so they (optimistically) forecasted big sales right out of the gate and produced a huge amount of inventory. Ultimately they had to give away vast quantities of the product and sent a large quantity of unused bottles to recycling.

KEEPING THE MAGIC ALIVE

At the same time Bloq was failing, Adam and Eric were realizing that the internal culture of the company was flailing.

The rapid growth of the company wore on its tight-knit family feel, and they were losing their fun culture that once came so naturally. So, they brought all the Method employees from their offices around the world to join them in one location for an offsite meeting. One of the goals was to get honest feedback about the state of the culture at Method. Adam and Eric did the best they could to create a space where their employees could be honest.

Some of the feedback showed a need for improvement at Method. People wanted more career development and more feedback, better on boarding, and more ongoing training. "Basically, people were asking for more structure, more process," says Anna Boyarsky, president of the Method Fan Club (aka advocacy director). "Process wasn't as necessary when we were smaller—our touch points were closer and the company was young and growing."

Adam and Eric wanted to create a company that would give the most amount of freedom to employees. The plan was to create as little structure as possible, thinking that it would create freedom. But the ironic thing is that, at a certain point in a company's growth, people crave structure, counterintuitively the structure enables the freedom. When there are clear guidelines for structure and expectations, then the employee is liberated to just focus all their energy on creating good work.

Adam and Eric knew that just creating a mission or a vision statement wouldn't be enough. Who ever remembers those things anyways? So they decided that the best thing to do was listen. They asked Method employees what they thought the Method culture was, then sat back and took notes. They filled notebooks. Upon returning to San Francisco, they pored through the notebooks to try to draw out some core values, then distill them without sucking the life out of them. They wanted to have solid core beliefs without the feeling of being institutional. "Our challenge as a company was, how do you keep the magic alive?" says Rudy Becker, the Resinator (aka engineering director). "It's one thing to succeed when you're small, but how do you keep all the good stuff while you grow? We knew what got us where we were and we didn't want to lose that. If we did lose it, it would almost not be worth it anymore."

They knew that their values had to articulate their purpose. So Method set up a team called "The Values Pod" to go through the process of articulating the core values of Method. This is what they came up with:

- Keep Method weird.
- What would MacGyver do?
- Innovate, don't imitate.
- Collaborate, collaborate, collaborate.
- Care like crazy.
- These five values are collectively called the Methodology.

Looking back, Adam and Eric would have spent time articulating their ideal culture from the outset, but they responded to the challenges and locked in their culture. If you go around the office, on the desk of most employees are five cards bound together by a ring. On each of those cards is one of the core values and the back of the card explains how to integrate that value into their work. The point is, the core values would always be on hand, not tucked away in the HR office.

THE LIMITS OF HUSTLE—TOUGH DECISIONS

Shortly after the failure of Bloq, the 2008 financial crisis hit, dampening their sales, and at the same time, they faced new competition from big home-care brands as they launched their own "green" cleaning products. Method was at a crucial juncture. Eric and Adam realized they had to rethink the way they were operating. And they had to do it fast.

At every other point in Method's growth, when they had been faced with challenges they had buckled down and worked harder and were able to pull through. When they needed to grow to 800 stores, they hustled and made it happen. When they needed to get the bottles produced for the launch in Target, they miraculously got it done. But the days of just working harder to get through a challenge were over. They were too big now for just some quick fix; they had to take a hard look at their operations and scale them back. This is one of the hardest things for any organizational leader to do, but it's especially difficult when the organization is your own creation. Failing to do so, though, will most likely result in the decline and ultimate failure of the company.

No matter how the finance team crunched the numbers, it was clear they were going to have to make major cuts to their staff to survive. The founders had always been open with employees about the company's finances, so everybody understood that cuts were going to have to be made, but that didn't make laying people off any easier. They decided they needed to lay off 10 percent of the workforce, and doing so was brutal.

They also decided they had to cut out the least profitable areas of their business. So, they killed their body care and air care lines, sold off the auto line, and stopped working with their least-profitable retailers. And they made a decision that many entrepreneurs must face once their companies have grown to a size that requires managerial expertise they don't have; they brought in an outside CEO with operational experience to lead the company through the crisis. These were all tough decisions, but they actually worked. By 2010, Method was back to strong profitability and growth.

Having weathered the crisis and bounced back, Method soon faced another of the common challenges of growth: the company was a prime target for takeover.

SELLING DOESN'T NECESSARILY MEAN SELLING OUT

In 2011 the company started getting inquiries from a number of large multinational soap companies. But Adam and Eric were determined that if they decided to sell, they would assure that the company continued to operate according to its founding principles. Many of the most successful social enterprises have been taken over by large corporations, and they've often been criticized for selling out. Honest Tea was acquired by Coke. Kashi was bought by Kellogg. Ben & Jerry's was sold to Unilever, prompting howls of disapproval from some fans. But if the acquiring company is itself in alignment with the mission, or if it is moving in the direction, a sale does not have to lead to an abandonment of the company's values and ways of operating; even its culture can be preserved.

In carefully considering the options, the Method founders and the board decided to sell to Ecover, the largest natural home care company in Europe, which has values similar to Method's. A Belgian company, it was founded in 1979 by a group of people who set out to create a phosphate-free laundry detergent.

The acquisition in May 2012 made Ecover the largest green cleaning company in the world, according to the company, and assured that Method products would continue to further the original mission.

The acquisition has brought Method into Europe, Asia, and Australia, and the larger scale allowed Ecover to build the first sustainable manufacturing facilities in Europe, as well as providing both the expertise and the financing for Method to build its first factory, a 150,000-square-foot LEED-certified soap production facility on Chicago's Far South Side, advancing Method's commitment to sustainable manufacturing.

Method was very fortunate to find a "green" company large enough to acquire them. But, even if a social enterprise is acquired by a major conglomerate without such an obvious mission alignment, the sale may result in accelerating the mission because the acquiring firm may not only provide resources and expertise that enable substantial growth, but may also internalize lessons from the social enterprise. Such has been the case with the sale of Burt's Bees.

A ROAD-SIDE STARTUP GOES CORPORATE

On Halloween 2007, a room full of employees waited for a secret announcement. Two men emerged at the front of the room dressed in bee costumes and revealed news that would alter the course of two companies.

The men in the bee costumes were a senior vice president from Clorox and the general manager of Burt's Bees. They were announcing Clorox's acquisition of Burt's Bees for the cool price of $925 million. The beloved all-natural products brand was joining the ranks of a company known for its chemicals.

Was Burt's selling out?

The sale seemed to come out of left field, but both companies had been deliberate about the partnership and had thought the strategy through carefully.

The new CEO of Clorox, Don Knauss, was interested in creating a more environmentally sustainable company. In addition, Clorox was turning 100 years old that spring and the executive management wanted to craft a forward-looking strategy that would refine, and to some extent redefine, what Clorox stands for. Knauss commissioned a study to assess how Clorox could respond better to its customers' needs as well as to the needs of the environment.

The research indicated that consumers are very concerned with their health and wellness and that of their families, and though they also value sustainability, it is of secondary concern. And Clorox customers cared more about their own home environment than the environment at large. That is to say that they prioritize the safety of their children in their daily routines at home over concerns about the impact of products on the environment. If a product will have a positive impact on the environment—or less of a negative impact—that's considered by most a nice plus. After studying the research, Clorox decided to place a new focus on creating healthier and more environmentally friendly products, which they had determined would differentiate them from their competitors and increase their market share.

One move was to create the Green Works product line of all-natural cleaning products. The company also wanted to invest in and acquire companies that aligned with the new strategy. Burt's Bees was a good candidate. The company was growing fast and Clorox knew that its massive distribution and marketing capabilities could greatly accelerate that growth. But the bigger question was mission alignment.

Would this acquisition alter the composition of the Burt's Bees product from natural to non-natural ingredients? Culture was another concern. There were many employees in that room on Halloween that were very concerned about how things would change after this small startup was acquired by a huge multinational. The questions and anxieties were certainly present. Was Clorox going to stay committed to this mission that they had established? Will Burt's Bees get diluted over time as it becomes part of a larger company?

Though there was some trepidation from the Burt's team, everyone was certainly aware of the potential for growth and expansion of the brand after acquisition.

Given the new resolve to be a sustainable company, and upon the acquisition of Burt's Bees, the Clorox CEO thought it was important to establish an internal ecostrategy office. He tapped an internal environmental champion, Bill Morrissey, to lead the newly established office. It wasn't rocket science. Bill looked at how Burt's had been operating since its inception and very quickly came to the conclusion that Burt's could serve as an internal exemplar for sustainability at Clorox.

Clorox was just setting up the Eco Team, and they had spent a good deal of effort reaching out to sources outside the company to learn best practices. But Burt's Bees would prove to be an especially valuable resource.

DUMPSTER DIVING

One example of how Clorox has learned from Burt's is in adopting a practice Burt's uses to reduce the waste it sends out into the world. Since 2010, Burt's has sent zero waste to landfills; the company is recycling, repurposing, or composting all of its waste. Clorox has taken a page from its book in working toward its own waste-reduction goals.

At 9:00 a.m. on a weekday, the Clorox Fairfield Bleach plant is usually humming with activity, in full-on production mode. Yet, this morning, not an employee was in the building. They were all in the parking lot, a crowd was gathered to watch as the dumpsters of the plant were upended and the nasty, smelly contents spilled across the parking lot. The employees, clad in coveralls and gloves, dove into the waste with vigor.

The "Dumpster Dive" was a long-standing established tradition at Burt's, and Clorox has adopted it. On Dumpster Dive day, all the employees sort through the trash in the parking lot to separate out recyclables and waste that can be composted. This one-day event is a tangible and effective tool that sensitizes the employees to become experts in waste management, all pulling toward the goal of zero waste to landfill. The average employee tends to be surprised at how much can be diverted from landfill, how much can be recycled, and how much can be composted.

But it is also essential that these events are not just one-off events, and the next day have life return to normal. So the employees meet that same day to devise action plans for further reducing waste. In the Fairfield plant, the employees had the idea of placing big recycling bins in seven different parts of the plant to make it convenient to sort the recyclable material and keep it out of the dumpster.

Every Clorox factory that has implemented the Dumpster Dive has seen an immediate 50 percent reduction in waste to landfills. Clorox has made a commitment of operating a dozen plants at zero waste to landfills by 2020. Currently, half a dozen are very close to achieving that goal.

A MORE SUSTAINABLE SUPPLY CHAIN

Another way in which Burt's has helped Clorox advance its sustainability goals is in bringing expertise in a natural supply chain management.

Clorox knew this was an area that they needed to improve on. In 2006, prior to the Burt's acquisition, Clorox had already dialed up its focus on sustainable sourcing. But they still had a long way to go in that area. By acquiring Burt's, they were acquiring one of the world's leading experts on sustainable sourcing.

One of the initial personnel changes after the acquisition was moving the sourcing manager from her role solely working on the Burt's Bees supply chain to her new role as a shared resource between Burt's Bees and Clorox as a whole. So she acts as a sort of internal management consultant to help reshape the sustainable supply chain practices across the company.

Prior to the addition of the new responsible sourcing manager, the primary focus of increasing sustainability in the Clorox supply chain was focused on how Clorox's own factories could be more sustainable in their production practices—the operational footprint, manufacturing, distribution footprint, and product portfolio. The question was how could Clorox make sustainability improvements to their products and production. Clorox began to make strides in that direction.

Clorox has been extremely efficient on its own manufacturing sites, "when you consider water and energy usage as well as greenhouse gas release. At Burt's we actually started adopting the rest of Clorox's goals in those areas because they're quite aggressive," says Paula Alexander.

The predominant attitude across the industry had been to take responsibility for what and how a company was producing their product, but to not ask too many questions about what the upstream suppliers and vendors were doing. Burt's Bees had never been satisfied with that standard and committed to taking responsibility for not only its own activities but how its suppliers and vendors were acting.

Companies like Burt's and Clorox are fundamentally formulators and marketers in consumer products. "People think of us a chemical company," says Morrissey. "We're not a chemical company. We buy our chemistry and our plastics from other suppliers upstream, but our responsibility doesn't end at our loading dock; we need to assume responsibility for the holistic product footprint from raw material to store shelf." Clorox has followed Burt's lead by making a commitment to ensure that its upstream suppliers are operating and sourcing in a sustainable manner.

The company started setting new goals to mandate a set of sustainability standards known as the Sustainability Vector for their top 200 suppliers, with the goal of the improving the sustainability of their suppliers by 80 percent. Additionally, Clorox is considering exchanging less-sustainable ingredients for more suitable ingredients in their products.

"So I would say that Burt's has been a great influence on sustainable sourcing," says Morrissey. "We have adopted a strategy that's maybe not as robust as theirs, but it's head and shoulders over what we've done in the past. We all know the sustainability journey is long. In the next six, seven years we can make great strides here, and that's our commitment."

LEARNING FROM THE BIG GUYS

The learning has also gone the other way. As the Clorox Eco Team continued to work toward the zero-waste goal, they determined the company should set a standard that 90 percent of the company's waste would be recycled or composted. And after hearing about Clorox's new standard, Burt's Bees decided to apply a stricter standard in its own plants.

This virtuous cycle of sharing best practices, adoption, and refinement is a great model for social enterprises that are acquired into larger companies to follow.

Burt's has benefited from the Clorox acquisition in other ways as well, and management has been careful to adopt practices and tap the new resources in ways that are true to the original mission. After the acquisition, Burt's was granted a great deal of autonomy. They knew the company could learn a great deal from Clorox, but they also knew they couldn't just copy and paste from the conglomerate. So, the team created a framework for evaluating how they would consider changes to make, called "Adopt, Adapt, or Invent," which set forth the following guidelines:

- Adopt—practices that are a good fit for their company and can be adopted as is from Clorox to Burt's. Many of the supply chain practices could be adopted directly and Burt's was able to take advantage of the economies of scale and systems in place for sourcing and manufacturing.

- Adapt—practices that are helpful, but need to be adjusted to meet the particular context. Some practices have a strong core concept, but cannot translate well from Clorox to Burt's Bees, so the team had to spend time adjusting and adapting the practice to meet their context. Most of the marketing practices were adapted for Burt's.

- Invent—when practices exist, but completely do not work in the given context, Burt's had to invent its own processes.

BECOMING MORE INNOVATIVE

Burt's has a goal that by 2020, 99 percent of the ingredients in the products will be natural. Clorox has helped the company work toward this goal by creating an innovative evaluation tool for making decisions about the sustainability of everything from ingredients to packaging and manufacturing.

Their "One Sustainability" program calculates a sustainability score for every new product. It allows the product development teams, at both Burt's and Clorox, to get hard data about the impact of all materials, ingredients, and packaging, and to compare their options on an apples-to-apples basis.

Burt's has also benefited greatly from the research and development resources and expertise Clorox has provided. The Burt's R&D team has been able to tap into technology used by Clorox to do some incredible things, such as adopting a technology used in making Hidden Valley salad dressings to make better skin lotions. Natural lotions are notoriously very liquidy, which inhibits their ability to moisturize. The Burt's Bees R&D team was able to tap into liquid salad dressing technology to create a good 24-hour moisturizing cream.

The focus on R&D and the sharing of knowledge between Clorox and Burt's Bees has also made the Burt's Bees products more natural. According to Paula Alexander, director of Sustainable Business and Innovation at Burt's, "over the past five years we've actually only grown more natural in our products. From 2009 to 2012, we went from 97 percent on average in terms of all natural to 99 percent. We now have almost 60 percent of our products at 100 percent natural.

Our packaging is only getting more sustainable as we push our-selves with more ambitious target setting."

There is often a negative response when a Colgate comes in and buys Tom's of Maine, or Unilever buys Ben & Jerry's or when Clorox comes in and buys Burt's Bees. There have been examples of the social and environmental impact being diluted or completely stripped out. In taking over Burt's, Clorox understood that its customers expect a natural product that is sustainable.

This not only makes sense from a purpose perspective, but also from a profit perspective. It's simply good business for Clorox. As Morrissey says, "We have been nothing but supportive of getting Burt's Bees to more natural, because that's their brand, that's what they are about. That's what they are going to be successful." The results have been quite successful indeed. Burt's Bee's revenues have grown by double digits every year (except for 2009) since the acquisition.

STICKING WITH STRENGTHS

The pressure to grow causes many founders to make another risky move: trying to extend into other sectors. The differences between even relatively similar markets can make taking on such new turf treacherous. For the Method team, just moving into a new category of cleaning substance proved an expensive mis-step. Expanding services can also be very tricky, because different communities have such different personalities and preferences and understanding those cultural factors is vital. One organiza-tion that has learned to stick with what it really knows is DonorsChoose.org.

In the first few years the organization grew organically, primar-ily through word of mouth. Teachers would post projects and get friends, family, parents to go to the site and fund them. But growth accelerated when DonorsChoose.org began to get a little attention in the media.

Charles was doing more cold calling to the media than he did to foundations. "The very first reporter not to just hang up on me was Jonathan Alter, who at the time who at the time was a senior editor at

Newsweek," said Charles. "He was kind enough to actually talk to me." Alter wrote a piece for the *Newsweek* web site saying that this experiment growing out of a Bronx classroom could one day change philanthropy.

Newsweek was the first real bit of news coverage. After much, much more cold calling the *New York Times* did a story about DonorsChoose.org. Word began to spread about this new concept of online philanthropy and donations picked up.

A little later, Jonathan Alter wrote a short paragraph piece in the print edition of *Newsweek* about DonorsChoose.org. One of Oprah Winfrey's producers saw it and she called Charles and had a conversation about the organization. A couple months later, a big limousine showed up outside of Wings Academy to pick Charles up and bring him to Oprah's show.

Charles didn't wait backstage very long at all. He recalls, "They sweep you onto the set very quickly without much like waiting, or to do. Oprah did this really awesome thing; she mentioned our web site address on air at the time. Typically if Oprah is going to highlight a web site, she'll tell people to go to Oprah.com and then find a link to that web site. She made an exception to that rule, and just told people to go to DonorsChoose.org directly. She came up to me in the green room afterward, and said that she'd made that exception since I was a teacher."

A month or two later that episode aired. At that moment, the best dream and worst nightmare for Charles happened simultaneously. As soon as Oprah mentioned the site, her army of followers flooded the site . . . and it crashed. Charles recalls, "We see nothing except for a crashed web site, which was excruciating. It took us a couple of hours to get back up. We knew that lots and lots of people were trying to donate and were coming to a crashed site." Eventually they got it back up and that day they raised $200,000.

As the platform proved to be successful, there was interest from other sectors to use the platform to fund projects outside the classroom. The first group to approach DonorsChoose.org was the New York Police Department. The concept was simple, just like teachers post projects to the site, police officers in New York City would be able to create project requests on DonorsChoose.org. The plan was to start out by focusing on community affairs officers and police officers that work with youth. These officers are on the front lines and understand the needs of each neighborhood. And, just like Charles' colleagues at Wings Academy, they had great vision and ideas, but no budget to implement.

Charles had taken the police officer exam his senior year of college, and had that his two choices were being either a teacher or a police officer. "So it was sort of personally exciting." In addition to Charles' personal excitement, the expansion aligned with their initial vision: to enable funding for any frontline public servant in New York City, including social workers, teachers, and police officers.

They had the funding to expand to the New York police department, and were about to launch the program. Then the deputy police commissioner who had been sponsoring this expansion was indicted by the FBI for absconding with foundations funds from another philanthropic foundation.

Charles recalls, "We all realized that we just had a serious brush with danger right there. Maybe we should stick to our knitting and focus solely on supporting public school teachers in the United States. To this day we do not have ambitions to extend to other sectors."

Instead of expanding into other sectors, DonorsChoose.org expanded geographically. Starting first in the Bronx, then the city of New York, then, slowly, going national. After Oprah they started getting inbound inquiries to expand to different markets across the country. The most persistent, passionate, and generous inquirer was from North Carolina. So, North Carolina was the first state in their national expansion. Generous philanthropists across America wanted to bring the platform to their cities and DonorsChoose. org followed the money, launching in Chicago, Los Angeles, and the San Francisco Bay area.

Around the same time Amazon was hosting the Nonprofit Innovation Award, a one-time award that Amazon held to identify the most innovative charity in America. Amazon had a panel of experts selecting 10 finalist organizations. Then the general public voted on which of those 10 finalists they felt was the most innovative. The final voting came down to Teach For America and

DonorsChoose.org. Charles recalls, "We couldn't quite believe that we—a pretty unknown charity—were neck in neck in the voting with Teach For America. We did a serious get out the vote drive, and we were lucky enough to win. It came with a big cash prize."

They had just earned a huge cash prize at the same time that the hurricanes hit New Orleans. They had a new pot of unrestricted funding and after Katrina and Rita hit, they saw an obvious need. So, for the first time, rather than just following the money, they created a strategic plan to open to public schools in all the states along the Gulf Coast—Texas, Mississippi, Louisiana, and Alabama. That was DonorsChoose.org's first large-scale expansion.

It took a round of major funding to bring the platform national to where it is today. "A lot of people see DonorsChoose.org and think 'Oh, that should be applied to social work in the United States, or to schools in India, or to lots of other sectors and countries.' Of course the amazing success of Kickstarter has only increased the number of people who are like, 'How should we apply micro giving, crowd funding, and project-based philanthropic marketplaces to my sector, or my country?' So the inquiries come every week," according to Charles. But they remain focused on helping to fix U.S. education, and have no plans to move beyond this focus. It's a good thing, because we have a long way to go here in the United States.

THE CHALLENGES OF A NEW LOCATION

Replicating a social enterprise while maintaining quality can be a daunting task. The social problems in most places around the country are much the same, but the local culture may make replicating a model that has worked so well in one place a frustrating and confusing struggle in another.

Often the founder and original team become stretched too thin to imprint the DNA of the organization's culture on the new team. The original team may often lacks the personal network in and knowledge of the new locations that are so important in gaining community buy-in. Additionally, organizations often choose new locations in a haphazard manner. This can lead to disconnects between the organization's mission and what the community in the new location wants and needs, or believes it needs. That is what Suzanne Mckechnie Klahr, the founder of BUILD, learned the hard way: when expanding into a new location you must have a strategic plan that starts with building community support.

Suzanne came to her idea for BUILD out of a deep immersion in the complex web of social problems she encountered working to assist small business owners in East Palo Alto with legal services. She had known for most of her life that she wanted to work to improve the lives of the poor, and she'd had some exposure to the issues, but East Palo Alto was a real eye-opener for her about both the inspiration and basic life skills she had received from her parents growing up, and the desperate need for more such support for children in poverty-stricken communities.

Her father was an immigrant who started with virtually nothing and became a successful businessman in New York City. Her mother was a public school teacher in Harlem, and during the 1980s when crack and the AIDS epidemic swept through the neighborhood Suzanne learned through her about the devastation it inflicted. That early exposure to two very different worlds—of business and public interest—and the tension she saw between them has shaped her path.

Suzanne decided she wanted to go into law, and she attended Stanford Law School during the dot-com boom of the 1990s, a heady time to be in Silicon Valley. Young entrepreneurs were raising millions of dollars in venture capital for sometimes-crazy ideas, some before even leaving college, and many became millionaires in a matter of just a few years. The market for lawyers to counsel these firms was strong.

Suzanne was torn. She wanted to learn corporate law well and build a network in the private sector, but she also wanted to leverage those skills and network to work on social justice issues. She took a position as a summer associate at Skadden Arps, a big white-shoe law firm, which she knew would be great experience no matter what kind of law she ended up practicing, and while she was there she learned about a Skadden fellowship that pays the recipient to do public interest work for up to two years. She applied and got the fellowship, and she began working in East Palo Alto, right down the road from Palo Alto, the beautiful and prosperous town that's home to Stanford, but a world away. At the time East Palo Alto was drug-ridden and the murder capital of the United States. She was working to provide legal services to small business owners. She was frustrated by how little difference she could make for them. The business owners had neither the personal networks nor the education and practical business skills they needed, and she saw that just helping them get funding and make their way through legal issues wasn't nearly enough support if they were going to make their businesses work. She learned about how the cycle of poverty stunted lives from so early on, limiting their opportunities and their perspective about what might be possible, and how it has undermined the commitment to education. Seventy percent of young people from the school district in which she was working were dropping out of high school.

One day four Latino boys approached her for help, telling her they wanted to drop out of high school and start a small business. She agreed to help them on the condition that they stay in school and improve their grades. Under her guidance, all four graduated from high school and entered college, and that experience inspired Suzanne to found BUILD. She realized that she could use the allure of learning about building a business to inspire students to work to get the education they needed to break out of the poverty cycle. The organization offers a four-year program for high school students in low-income communities, teaching them about entrepreneurship, and helping them find jobs, while also building their life skills and encouraging and preparing them to go to college.

She has put a strong emphasis on helping children to believe in themselves and to learn the fundamental skills that have been found to be central to later success in life, such as grit and resilience. Unlike many youth entrepreneurship programs, in which kids start a business on their own, BUILD has them work in teams, which both provides the support of friends working on the same problems and encountering the same challenges and teaches them vital lessons about collaboration and conflict resolution.

In getting BUILD off the ground, Suzanne soon realized that rather than operating as an after-school enrichment program, BUILD would be more effective if the program was built into the normal school day, becoming part of the curriculum. She learned that while after-school programs can work well for high-potential kids who are already motivated, for the more disadvantaged and disengaged students that were her target audience getting them to attend after school can be very difficult. Getting the agreement of the school district management and teachers was no small feat, and she was able to do so in large part because she had gotten to know the community so well. Year after year BUILD continued to have more and more impact in East Palo Alto. Then BUILD slowly started expanding to neighboring communities in the Bay area.

YOUR REPUTATION MAY PRECEDE YOU, BUT YOU NEED COMMUNITY SUPPORT

In expanding, BUILD first moved right across the bay to Oakland, which went quite smoothly because there was so much awareness in the community about the success of the original program. But the next step, all the way to the East Coast, was a real challenge, and the launch there nearly failed. Suzanne recalls, "I knew that I wanted BUILD to the East Coast, but didn't know much about scaling."

She decided to open in Washington, D.C., because an early employee of BUILD expressed interest in heading up expansion there. She had left BUILD to go to graduate school and had moved to D.C. thereafter.

She and Suzanne thought that they could fairly readily take the model that had been working so well in the Bay Area and transplant it. Suzanne looks back on the experience with the humility that can only come from experience, noting, "Just parachuting someone in to serve the community is never going to be as impactful as first learning about what the community needs and bringing local champions on board." The D.C. office struggled to gain the traction with the community that can make or break such an effort—the school board, the teachers, local business leaders, and the political leadership. Developing that support took two difficult years, but finally the program took hold.

When the opportunity to expand to Boston presented itself, Suzanne knew the approach had to be more intentional. She determined to start by creating school partnerships as well as launching an awareness and fund-raising campaign in advance. The organization tendered a Request for Proposal, inviting schools to vie for the opportunity to host BUILD, expecting to start with two schools. But the response was so strong, with 17 schools inviting BUILD in, that they decided to start with four.

Suzanne was also careful to select a leader, Ayele Shakur, who was from the community and had a strong local network, which lent a great deal of credibility and expertise to both the launch of the programs and the fund-raising efforts. By doing this groundwork, making sure to cultivate local champions, pre-partnering with schools, and fundraising in advance to provide adequate financial support for the organizational infrastructure needed, BUILD Boston got off to a much stronger start.

KEY TAKEAWAYS

Growth is never easy. There are many mistakes to be made along the way, and that is to be expected. Even the most successful entrepreneurs will tell you they have endured a great many setbacks. The biggest difference in getting through the challenges, in addition to founders being resilient and open-minded about changes that must be made, is drawing on the strength of community building. Social enterprises have an advantage in growing communities of support because they can highlight their purpose, but this in no way means people will just fall in line. And you've got to carefully monitor whether you are staying true to your mission and are not letting your community down, both the community you create within the organization and the supporters you bring in from the community at large, first and foremost your customers or target market.

Founders must be highly strategic in making decisions about expansion, and staying true to the mission and to the vision and experience that helped you to create a successful organization in the first place is crucial in this process. You must carefully consider how any given new product or service will line up with the mission and how your experience will allow you to do a good job of developing it.

Finally, you must do lots of legwork and market testing and preparation before you implement any brand extension or expansion to new terrain, no matter how much of a sure bet it seems.

There are three key things you must to do manage smart growth.

1. Articulate

Much as adolescents who become all but unknowable to their parents, growing organizations can forget their identity. Writing organizational values and a mission statement may seem superficial, but they can act as powerful guard rails to keep you from swerving away from your mission, and to assure that all employees understand your purpose and how important it is to you.

Key Question: What are the values that will drive the growth of my organization and how will they contribute to the connection with the organization's community of support?

2. Systemize

Nurturing a culture that exemplifies those values and the spirit of purpose you want to infuse into the organization requires putting processes in place to maintain the culture. But nobody wants to have their organization bogged down by endless reports and paperwork. You must find a way to set up good procedures and monitor employee engagement and productivity while keeping your organization nimble, focused on the mission, and true to its values.

The weekly 5-15 report is one great method, but each founder should think this issue through for herself and create procedures that are right for her particular organization.

Key Question: What key practices should I put in place to align my actions and those of my staff with the organization's mission and values?

3. Expand Purposefully

Not all growth is created equal. There's dumb growth and smart growth. Smart growth is guided by strategy and disciplined vision. Founders must not simply jump at opportunities that present themselves. Having a purpose is one of the most powerful sources of guidance in distinguishing which opportunities make sense and are worth taking some risk for, and which you should forgo.

Key Question: Is this new initiative I'm considering purposeful and thoughtful, or would it be a case of just growing to grow?

CHAPTER SEVEN

Evaluate with Honesty

Good social innovators want to know that they are making progress toward their mission. If they cannot rely on the accuracy of data they may well steer the organization in the wrong direction, and they may also fail to attract continuing funding. Honest evaluation of impact, ideally with hard data, is a means to prove that an organization is living up to its values as well as to guide founders about what programs and products to continue developing and which to set aside.

BAKING METRICS INTO YOUR PROCESS

D-Rev's *user obsession* goes way beyond the design process. Once the product is in the users' hands, they want to know how it's being used and have a clear idea of what impact it will create.

D-Rev is working on a budget of less than a million dollars a year, and they have three projects currently running, plus R&D and impact assessment. So, when it comes to evaluation, they have to get it done on a shoestring budget. The name of the game for them is *efficiency*. How can they collect the most relevant information tied directly to impact in a streamlined, efficient manner.

Early in the design process they clearly define the goal of each project, and then they develop metrics to measure effectiveness in reaching it. For instance, with Brilliance their metrics are number of babies treated, number of babies treated that would otherwise not have been treated, and finally deaths and disabilities averted.

With the Knee, the metrics are number of amputees fit and number of amputees wearing the Knee six months after being fit.

The team is looking to add a new metric, which will quantify the raise in income after wearing the Knee.

D-Rev builds the gathering of this data into its products. So, with Brilliance the device actually stores the total time that it's in use. That data is sent to the D-Rev office. Since they know the average treatment time, they can arrive at a very solid estimate of babies treated, and then based on the characteristics of a hospital, they can determine if those babies would have likely been treated otherwise. They take this data and cross reference it against the medical literature to arrive at number of deaths and disabilities averted.

D-Rev defines success by impact, not simply by units sold. Many organizations simply guess at impact by taking the number of devices disseminated and multiplying that number by a guess at how many people that device can serve. Krista Donaldson says, "We fundamentally want to know if we're reaching our impact goals. I've been in countless hospitals, with devices sitting in the corner still in wrappers that haven't been opened because nobody knows how to use them. Or they run on a different voltage system. Then also I've seen devices, they've been plugged in and there is the voltage surge that fries them within the first 10 minutes. We want to make sure that our devices are in use, and they are being used properly. That's why we are doing this work. We need to know if we're actually doing it well."

Building evaluation into the product allows you to understand if the product is being used and whether it's being used properly. For instance, D-Rev is able to see where Brilliance is being used within the hospital or clinic. In some cases the device was being used in the neonatal care unit where an incubator is necessary. But in other cases it was being used in the hospital ward with the mothers, where incubators are not necessary. The team is using this data to evaluate whether or not to create a stripped-down version of the product for the use of mothers in the wards.

CONSIDERED DESIGN

Under the Corporate Social Responsibility regime, Nike had embedded environmental teams into both footwear and apparel in order to assess the environmental impact of the product.

Designers designed the product then shipped it to the developers. The developers would make the plan for the factory, then ship it to the factory. The factory would manufacture the product. Then, at the end, just as the product was about to be shipped to the stores, the environmental team would do the assessment and say that that the product was good or bad. Sustainability was not much more than an afterthought. This process put evaluation too late in the process to be meaningful. It's like looking in the rearview mirror while driving. It doesn't help anybody, and in fact it's just irritating to the designers, producers, and manufacturers.

Hannah Jones saw this issue, and understood that if they kept that same process, sustainability was an afterthought, a box that is checked, but has little impact on the end product. So, she got together with John Hock, VP of design, and Mark Parker, the CEO, who came out of the design team, told them the issue, why the status quo wasn't working, and said, "We've got to pivot here." They agreed.

When Nike launched Considered Design, Mark Parker said to the company, "If all we do is create a green product line then we have failed. Considered is an ethos for the company. Sustainability is an ethos." For Nike, the product needs to perform, period. Or it is irrelevant. Hannah says, "The consumer loves great product, and my job is to provide the consumer with great product, that by the way is breakthrough sustainability."

She continued, "So when the athlete puts on his Flyknit and he wins a gold in the Olympics, he wins because they are the lightest, most form-fitting shoes he has worn before in his life, and 'Oh, by the way there is a 70 percent reduction in waste.' So to me, I don't really mind what the consumer thinks about sustainability because what I care about is my athlete. What I care about is performance, and sustainability is part of our promise to you, as a brand, to enable your performance. The SB&I team refuses to compromise performance in their journey toward innovative sustainability."

So, Hannah made a couple of major changes. First, she hired a new team lead. The new team lead wasn't an environmentalist or a material scientist—he was an industrial designer. He understood how the design process worked. Hannah gave him a challenge, "We said now go do something that is going to be useful for designers, so that in the very moment of designing and developing the product they can actually problem solve, change the materials they use, and think about design differently." By the time the products go into the factory sustainability has been baked into it.

In order for this to matter, the team needed to be physically moved from the end of the supply chain to the design process. So the team was merged together and placed up front in the design team. They challenged the design team to think like designers, not compliance officers.

Once the move happened, and the design and sustainability teams started to work together in the design process, it became clear that in order for this to work the designers needed to have a clear and easy way of understanding the sustainability of each material.

They started researching all the materials in their database. Nike is a big company making products all over the world with thousands of materials. Creating a lifecycle analysis on each material is a huge task. It took them seven years to catalog and assess all of the materials. Each material was given an overall environmental score that would help designers to make decisions. A low score indicates poor sustainability and a high score indicates that it is sustainable.

Designers use the tool and are given a decision in the design process. For instance, if the designer wanted to use cotton, they have a choice between the types of cotton and a clear, simple way to assess good cotton from better cotton: material with low toxicity rather than high toxicity; material with a small water footprint rather than one with a large water footprint. If the designer is going to use a material that has a relatively low score, take nylon for instance, then they are challenged to manipulate the design in such a way to increase material efficiency.

"The point is," Hannah says, "you are giving them real-time solutions that then can go to scale across the company. And you create a bit of an internal competition as well, because each designer innovates and thinks about really cool new ways to do things more sustainably."

All of the designs, tricks, and tips are indexed back into the database and help other designers learn from the incremental design process and material innovation. The database becomes a sort of internal wiki—a living document on sustainable design innovation.

THROW IT OVER THE WALL

If you walk into a factory in Asia producing footwear, you will see one line producing Nike, one line producing Puma, and another line producing Adidas. The factories crank out hundreds of thousands of pairs of shoes annually for all of the big brands. They are huge operations.

So, any social or environmental innovation by one brand would only affect one line in a factory, creating an oasis in the middle of the desert. Furthermore, that one brand would bear the cost of lonely leadership, increasing their costs and giving them a competitive disadvantage. It was clear that Nike didn't just want internal change, but in order for this change to be effective they needed to affect system change.

In 2006 the first big move they made was deciding to disclose the factory locations, in order to improve monitoring of working conditions. Up to that point, the entire industry considered the very location of their contracted factories to be a trade secret.

So Hannah and the head of sourcing made the case for disclosure. She said, "If we were to disclose the factory locations it would trigger collaboration in monitoring and remediation. It would scale our collective ability as an industry to enforce labor standards." The discussion went all the way to the board. Hannah found herself in a board meeting listening to their deliberation on the issue, listing the pros and cons. This had never been done before by anybody. But, eventually the board agreed that if it improved working conditions across factories it would be the right thing to do. "So we came out with it," said Hannah, "we just disclosed."

That disclosure triggered the head of the Trade Union Movement to run a campaign supporting what they had done and asking other brands to do the same thing. Imagine that, the very organizations that had been leading campaigns against Nike a few years earlier were now leading campaigns promoting them.

Today a large number of the apparel and footwear industry members have disclosed their supply chains and work together more closely and more effectively through the Fair Labor Association. Now that they know where the different factories are located, there is more efficiency and coverage in the monitoring process, instead of having six monitors go to one factory in Turkey, but not to one in Bangladesh. There is now clarity, which results in effective monitoring.

Additionally, the disclosure of their factory locations had no impact whatsoever on Nike's competitiveness. That fear proved to be unfounded. So, it was a win for sustainability in that it created larger system change, without any negative affect on the business.

"That was a pivot point to us as well as a lesson learned," says Hannah. "Sometimes you have to take risk. You have to do something that is very counterintuitive, being transparent and open. But if it is done thoughtfully, it can trigger real system change."

That experience began the process of moving from internal innovation to open innovation that catalyzes system change. Within SB&I there is somebody whose job it is to think about the next trigger for a system change through open innovation. When do they keep innovation within the walls of Nike? When do they open it up and throw it over the wall? Hannah says, "We have a very clear approach. We look at all of our work and we say is it pre-competitive or is it competitive? So everything that is competitive we lock down just as we do with every innovation. Everything that is pre-competitive we take it out into the world and change the system and make it a new norm, while rendering the old way of doing things obsolete."

Nike's Considered Design is a great example of pre-competitive innovation. They are not sharing some newly patented fabric or construction process, which would be competitive. Instead they are simply sharing an easy tool for designers to understand the sustainability impact of their design choices.

The materials database, which was worth millions of dollars and took seven years of hard work to build, was thrown over the wall— opened up to the public, for anyone to use.

Nike created the federative Wiki of materials, which was built by the guy that actually wrote the code for Wikipedia. Hannah says, "He lived with us for a year. It was an awesome mash up of talent in the office. He actually turned the database into a Wiki that anybody could access. The format of an evolving Wiki was the right choice for this project because it's the science that's always evolving, and new materials are always coming forward."

Nike gave the Wiki to a trusted neutral party, the Sustainable Power Coalition, in order to encourage everyone in the industry to use it. Now this innovation that started inside the walls of Nike is available for people to continuously update a single Wiki of sustainability footprint of different materials.

Though the information was out, free to the world through the Wiki, it was still a bit clunky and took some practice to use it well. Hannah realized that just the information needed to be simplified and packaged in a more user-friendly platform. Hannah said, "So we had all these databases, but how do I make this simple? How do I make this intuitive? How do I make it something so sticky that every designer in the world is going to want to use this?"

So, they decided to take the Wiki to the London College of Fashion and host a hackathon. They gathered a bunch of coders and gave them a challenge of transforming the data into something delightful. The result of the hackathon was the concept for the Materials App.

The Materials App puts the entire database in the designers' pockets and allows them to see how their design choices affect the sustainability of the garment. The app is designed with a simple user interface that is highly intuitive. The idea is you can be any designer anywhere—whether you are an independent designer, or work at a major fashion house—and you can quickly start to make smarter choices when you are designing, because of your ability to access the information in an intuitive app that's always with you because it's on your smartphone. The Materials app is built on an open API, and Nike encourages people to riff on the app and play with different ways to present the data. Hannah says the beauty of the Materials app is that "you can move designers in the movement to be the ones that drive sustainable decision making the moment when they touch their design table or computer."

The app hit their download target within two weeks. But Hannah is quick to point out that, "We are not trying to get to the big numbers because that is not the point. The point is to get to the designers that will use it."

Nike is now working in partnerships with six European fashion colleges, and a few in the United States to embed the app in their curriculums in an attempt to bake sustainable decision making into the design process for the next generation of designers.

For Nike, the choice of materials is essential because the materials they use create 60 percent of their environmental footprint. The materials vendors are huge. Nike alone is not big enough to create systems change with the material producers because they have so many other customers..

"We fundamentally believe that if you can change the world's materials, you can literally change the world," says Hannah. "So when you think about it, if we don't create a road map to a better future, and then bring the rest of the industry with us, we are not going to get the change we need in the time we need."

There is a real urgency to Hannah's vision for transforming her industry through evaluation. She is not content to talk about how to effect system change. In typical Nike fashion she says you need to "JUST DO IT."

MEASURING YOUR FOOTPRINT

In order to evaluate its environmental performance, Method focuses on their waste, water, and material usage. Adam says, "We have a series of metrics that we use, things like carbon footprinting. There are well-established metrics for that now, like through the Global Reporting Initiative and Carbon Disclosure Project." They also measure their energy usage and the embedded energy in all of the materials they buy. In addition, they measure 100 percent of their waste and whether it goes into recycling or landfills. They also meter their water use, and they recycle 100 percent of the water used in manufacturing.

And they don't stop there. They also measure their social performance. They decided to apply for B Corporation certification and they use those social and environmental metrics. They are also transparent with the public about their progress. By visiting the company web site, anyone can see their full social and environmental report. It is essentially a real-time, fully transparent online sustainability report.

LEARNING TO LOVE DATA MINING

The team at DonorsChoose.org are data geeks. They are the type of people that get excited about a daily email containing metrics, benchmarks, and daily, weekly, and year-over-year comparisons of performance and impact. It's the type of organization that has a data scientist on staff. Have you met any other for-purpose organizations with a data scientist? Neither have I.

Every day the data scientist sends a dashboard to everybody in the organization. On the dashboard are statistics like year-over-year growth in new donors, repeat donors, and donors acquired by teachers fundraising for their own projects. The dashboard includes things like year-over-year growth in dollars donated from credit cards to classroom projects on our site, year-over-year growth in active teachers, and percent of high-poverty public schools using the site. All of those statistics are crunched every morning.

These statistics show a baseline of how effective the platform is at getting classroom projects funded, helping the staff stay focused on the mission. The dashboard also provides a daily assessment of the vibrancy of their philanthropic support. But beyond that, Charles is interested in some higher-order questions about the ultimate impact of the public's engagement in the program on retaining great teachers, as well as in evaluating how well DonorsChoose.org is leveling the playing field when it comes to the resources available to classrooms in low-income communities.

Studies have shown clearly that the most significant factor in a child's learning is the quality of teachers. Charles says "I think that people agree that the all-important question is, how do we recruit more great teachers, and how do we keep more great teachers." He hopes DonorsChoose.org can play a real role in keeping great teachers.

By measuring data from teacher surveys, they have already demonstrated that those teachers who use the site post substantially greater-than-average student test score gains. Charles says, "Our site self selects for kickass teachers. We've demonstrated that." What he hopes to be able to show eventually is that the site has a causal impact on keeping teachers in the classroom because they get the resources they need. He hopes the site makes them feel liberated to be innovators, to devise awesome projects, and to make them feel that people all over the country are rooting for them.

In terms of evaluating the impact of the funded projects on educational outcomes, their data scientist digs through the data, controlling for the fact that the site self-selects for motivated teachers. In one analysis, he isolated a control group of teachers who registered on DonorsChoose.org and took the initiative to create a project that was good enough to get posted, but were not funded. So theoretically, those teachers are highly engaged. Then he isolated another group comprised of teachers who posted projects that were funded. The concept is that teachers in both groups are highly engaged, and likely very good teachers. The only difference is that one group was funded and the other was not. His evaluation of such results is ongoing.

The evaluation methods aren't perfect, but the data is always enlightening. DonorsChoose.org also conducts teacher surveys to ask about the impact of funded projects on students' academic achievement, on interest in learning, and on students' sense that there are people out there who care about them and are invested in their educational success. "The positive feeling that comes with knowing that there are people in a student's community or at large that care about them enough to invest is often the most pronounced change that teachers report," Charles says.

HACKING EDUCATION

When the site first launched, donors engaged with it very much as they would with any marketplace site, just browsing page after page of projects without any particular criteria. According to Charles, "People are not used to expressing their particular passion when they're making a charitable gift. Let's say that you have a personal passion for woodworking and a personal passion for J.D. Salinger. We've got woodworking, and J.D. Salinger projects on our site that would make you light up." The desire to exercise personal choice and expression is top of mind as we consume—fashion, home wares, even Method soap—but it rarely crosses our mind when giving. Most donors have never been asked to do that. Charles wanted to create a platform that helped donors find projects they are particularly passionate about in the same way that Netflix and Amazon serve up options for the viewer or shopper.

So first he redesigned the site to feature projects by subject area, like art and science. But later he got a more innovative idea for engaging donors on the site. He decided to open up the data to the public by created an API that anybody can tap into and play with. In order to encourage hackers to use the data creatively, he created a competition for the most creative app based on their API.

Thus was Hacking Education born.

Hacking Education is a challenge for hackers to use their skills to improve the giving experience for donors. Every app, plug-in, or site developed is open to the public to use. Chris decided to make the program a competition and he appointed an expert judging panel to select a winner. The submissions were smart and creative. Vincent Dibartolo used geographic data to create an app that allows runners to fund a project when they run by a specific school and allows friends and family to pledge a certain dollar amount per mile toward a classroom project. Kevin Marshall created a project-recommenda- tion engine based on what a donor is saying on Twitter. Michael Nutt was the big winner for creating a dynamic email signature that promotes your current DonorsChoose.org project to everybody you email. The competition also turned out to be great for publicity. Nutt was invited onto the Colbert Report and got a hearty endorsement from the normally sarcastic Colbert, who said "You're really smart."

After the fun and success of Hacking Education, Charles thought it would be good to open up the data not just for apps and hacks, but for serious research. "We're seeing more research now that we have opened up all of our data," he says. "So anybody can geek out on our data. They can run a regression analysis to see the resources most requested by Louisiana high school teachers or trending topics and themes and projects created by kindergarten teachers nationally."

The goal with opening up their data is to create systemic change in the American education system by enabling people to make discoveries about what resources teachers most need in particular communities. School leadership may be able to create better classroom experiences and policy makers might be able to use the data to craft smarter education legislation. At least that's what Charles hopes.

THE BIGGER YOU ARE, THE MORE DATA YOU HAVE

Though there are challenges with attempting to innovate within large corporations, there are some advantages as well, including financial support, distribution networks, and clout that can be used to rally partners. But one of the largest built-in advantages is the culture of evaluation and data-driven decision making. A large corporation like Coca-Cola is obsessive about measuring the performance of every sector of its business

According to Bea Perez, Chief Sustainability Officer of The Coca-Cola Company, in the normal course of Coca-Cola's business, "We are very data driven. We have a lot of discipline and rigor around data. We look at data on a daily basis. We look at volume, profit, operating income. I mean the basic things that we report on our quarterly earnings. We have to know how is it totaling every day, every week, every month, in order to ensure performance at the end of the quarter."

Many large corporations have a rigorous data-driven approach to squeezing the most profit out of each quarter that they possibly can, but when it comes to social innovation, they seem to take their data-driven hat off. So decisions that are made around social innovation or anything in the "do good" category are made intuitively, with no clear data to support them, no clear objectives, and no evaluation metrics in place.

For Bea this is an anathema. Why should a company change its data-driven approach just because the objectives are about social or environmental impact rather than pure profit? In fact, the need for clear goals and evaluation on social/environmental goals is likely more important because the impact may be less evident to senior leadership of the company. Bea says, "At Coca-Cola that data-driven perspective doesn't change when we're talking about sustainability. It's typically more long term. But there are key indicators that you know you're making progress or not."

At the beginning of any partnership Bea runs a process of establishing clear objectives. Since most of Coca-Cola's projects are done as partnerships, it is essential to have an honest assessment about what everyone is looking to get out of it. What is the objective for every business? What's the objective of the partnership and then ultimately of the project in the initiatives being driven? They implement a two-step process of defining each partner's objectives and then defining the objective of the overarching project. This process is conducted at the very beginning to avoid ambiguity.

For EKOCYCLE, the overarching goal of the project is to increase recycling. In order to measure that, Coca-Cola looks at recycling rate. But beyond that, they also dig deeper and measure intent to recycle. They want to move the needle on both, so they have the metrics and the measurement tools in place on a continuous basis to see if the needle is being moved, and how long it takes to move the needle.

At the same time, Coca-Cola measures the impact on its brand as well as Will.I.Am's brand. According to Bea, "It's really important to state very clearly upfront, making sure that everyone is clear on the objective, the role that each partner plays, and then how to measure and track that. So we can have consistent data year over year to say are we making progress."

In order for EKOCYCLE to mean anything, there must be integrity in the manufacturing process. So, for their manufacturing partners like Beats or Levi, they set a minimum threshold of performance that is expected and they follow up with audits to ensure performance— their version of the trust-but-verify approach. "We look at what they've publically reported on sustainability and we show them best practices we've seen," says Bea. "Then we do the audit."

Changing manufacturing processes is not an easy or cheap undertaking. Sometimes brands are giving an honest effort, but once the audit team makes a visit to the factories it's clear that they have not made enough progress. In those circumstances, Bea gives them clear criteria and a period of time to change, but if they don't change EKOCYCLE can't use them as a partner.

The data helps them understand if they are making progress and where the challenges are. If they are not making progress, then Bea asks, "How do we pivot it in order to make progress, just like any good entrepreneur would do. You have to have some flexibility as you learn and adjust your plan, in order to get that learning to drive better results."

Real-time evaluation is important for Coca-Cola because they want to know that they are doing what they said they'd do. Because as Bea notes, "We're very firm on keeping our commitments, and making sure that we're truly delivering on expectations." But this level of evaluation allows you to make informed decisions as the project progresses so that if there's a problem, they can identify it early and pivot to get back on track.

But in order for EKOCYCLE to really change paradigms they are also evaluating consumer sentiment. Beyond brand awareness, they want to know if they like the brand and think that it matches with their values and vision for how they define purpose. Is it going to get them to recycle more? Do they think it's cool? Will they recommend it to other people? What are the sales of the EKOCYCLE, by brand.

"Success," Bea says, "is that the brand does what it was intended to do, which is to create awareness around recycling and that people change behavior. They change attitude and behaviors, and that we see those areas increase around the world. How do we continue to drive success not just for our brands but for those partner brands? How do we think about scaling this as we get information, and improve upon what we know? Driving scale is also critical to us as well as we think about long-term success."

First things first, EKOCYCLE is still only a couple years old, so they are still pushing toward milestones set out at the beginning of the project. But, once they have been achieved, "Then we think about scaling this to get it more broadly accepted." EKOCYCLE will, in the long term, measure its success by changing behaviors, both at the consumer and manufacturing level.

COLLECTING DATA OVER TIME

Measuring the progress of their students has always been an essential part of BUILD. Success in the classroom as well as in business is dependant upon many variables, so in order to shape a program that has results, the more data you have the better.

BUILD measures a tremendous amount of data. It is a data-driven organization. They collect demographic personal data, school data, academic performance data, attendance, retention, grades, ability to do well on a pre and post test, participation in the business plan competition, performance in the business plan competition, number of colleges applied to and accepted to, financial aid received. In addition to the hard data, they also have created assessments to understand how the students score on collaboration, self-efficacy, and resilience. And this is only some of the data collected.

The team looks at all of this data and attempts to isolate what variables have the most impact. In the beginning the BUILD team tracked everything on a single Microsoft Excel spreadsheet. "You can imagine having all of the students' names, and having to scroll over 100 columns for all of their attendance, and all of their retention information, and their grades, and everything happening," says Suzanne.

A few years ago, they moved to a CRM system built on the Sales Force platform called Athena, after the goddess of wisdom and war. This new system allowed them to sort data much better and isolate the data points that created the most impact.

Now, they have begun to simplify their use of data. "What we are realizing is that we have collected too much, and that we now need to scale back the amount of data that we are collecting, to really focus on those data points, the ones that we can move a needle on," Suzanne says.

With Athena they are able to track a tremendous amount, but only display the essential data for decision making. "You don't want to have your program people swimming in so much data and having to collect so much and track so much that they are not able to do the work that needs to happen. So we are going through a revision process right now to scale back, and make sure the data we are collecting is data that is the most critically important, for what's going to drive impact and outcomes for our students," says Suzanne.

When it comes to data collection, it's quality not quantity that helps with effective decision making. So BUILD has now implemented a dashboard system that will allow its managers at a glance to inform their daily practice on the variables that are important to their specific roles.

Over the long term, BUILD is conducting longitudinal studies of its students so that they can keep track of the lifelong impact on those students. Using smart data evaluation, they will be able to assess how their intervention in a young person's life has changed the overall trajectory.

KEY TAKEAWAYS

As you design your organization and grow it, you should look for every opportunity to gather as much data as possible with which to evaluate your impact. In addition to having data to back up your claims of social and environmental performance with key stakeholders, measurement helps you gain feedback and constantly iterate toward better performance. But there is good data analysis and bad data analysis. You've got to have well-thought-out metrics. There are a few best practices for this.

1. Measure What Matters

When it comes to blending profit and purpose, both need to be measured. Vague ideas of profitability or social good are not sufficient for leading for-purpose organizations. There are so many organizations out there that are green-washing or social-washing—talking about doing good, but not actually making any impact—that for-purpose organizations need to distance themselves from this crowd. A key means of differentiation is by proving impact through objective data.

Here are a number of good methods to use.

- Balanced Scorecards: The balanced scorecard is a strategic planning and management system. A simple definition of a Balanced Scorecard is a focused set of key financial and non-financial indicators. These indicators include both leading and lagging measures. The term *balanced* does not mean equivalence among the measures, but rather an acknowledgement of other key performance metrics that are not financial. The now-classic Balanced Scorecard, as outlined by Robert Kaplan and David Norton, has four quadrants or perspectives:

- people and knowledge,
- internal,
- customer, and
- financial

For example, increased training for employees (people and knowledge) can lead to enhanced operations or processes (internal), which leads to more satisfied customers through either improved delivery time and/or lower prices (customers), which finally leads to higher financial performance for the organization (financial).

- Social Return on Investment (SROI): SROI is an approach to understanding and managing the value of the social, economic, and environmental outcomes created by an activity or an organization. It is based on a set of principles that are applied within a framework. SROI seeks to include the values of people that are often excluded from markets in the same terms as used in markets—money—in order to give people a voice in resource-allocation decisions. SROI is a framework to structure thinking and understanding. It's a story, not a number. The story should show how you understand the value created, manage it, and can prove it.

- ESG: ESG stands for Environmental, Social, and Governance. It is a measurement used in many large corporations and is also often used by portfolio managers trading those corporations. There is growing evidence that suggests that ESG factors, when integrated into investment analysis and decision making, may offer investors potential long-term performance advantages. ESG factors offer portfolio managers added insight into the quality of a company's management, culture, risk profile, and other characteristics.

- Social Accountability 8000 (SA8000): The SA8000 standard is the central document of the work at SAI. It is one of the world's first auditable social certification standards for decent workplaces, across all industrial sectors. It is based on conventions of the ILO, UN, and national law, and spans industry and corporate codes to create a common language to measure social compliance. It takes a management-systems approach by setting out the structures and procedures that companies must adopt in order to ensure that compliance with the standard is continuously reviewed. Those seeking to comply with SA8000 have adopted policies and procedures that protect the basic human rights of workers.

- B Corp Certification: B Corp certification is a voluntary certification for sustainable business that validates a company's social/environmental performance. A company has to meet rigorous standards of social and environmental performance and transparently disclose its performance to the world on its web site. If it passes the assessment and complies with the requirements, then the company becomes one of the B corp-certified companies.

   The B Corp certification shows the world that as you grow you are serious about keeping purpose at the core of your business.

Aside from external tools, it often makes sense to create custom measurement tools to serve the right data to the right decision maker in the organization, which will allow them to make data-driven decisions. No matter whether you are creating your own custom performance standards or using a third-party performance standard, you must decide on specific pieces of data that truly move the needle toward the desired outcome and maintain a relentless focus on improving performance against that metric. Long-term consistent growth does not happen accidentally, it is the result of a clear focus of energy on the most important activities to make progress in order to make smart data-driven decisions. That is measuring what matters.

Key Question: What are the most important metrics for me to measure in order to drive the organization toward the desired social/environmental goals?

2. Measure Throughout the Process

After identifying what to measure and the measurement tools, the question remains, *when* should you measure. Evaluation can often be an afterthought. With limited time and resources available, evaluation of performance can easily take a lower priority to seemingly more pressing matters. But measurement is essential to stay on track and continually improve, so it must be prioritized, not at the end of the process, but throughout the entire process.

When evaluation is happening throughout the value-creation process, you are able to track real-time performance and make small adjustments along the way. You also avoid any surprises that may emerge when there is infrequent evaluation. By measuring throughout the process, you gain a wealth of data to use in making both short-term and long-term decisions. The more data points you have, the more you're able to understand and communicate your impact story, both within the organization and outside.

Key Question: At what points in the value creation process should I be measuring my social/environmental performance?

3. Be Transparent

In order to effect system change, sometimes it's important to open up the data you have collected to public scrutiny, and to let other organizations use it to make decisions.

Transparency is impressive to investors and funders, and it also reassures the public at large about the authenticity of your commitment to your mission. And the more that organizations share the data they're gathering, the more we can all learn from it.

Key Question: What is the appropriate data for our organization to share externally in order to create systemic change?

Conclusion

I find long conclusions annoying, so I'll make this one short.

In all the conversations I've had with successful founders of social enterprises and in all of the work I've done with them, the most pronounced factor in their success has been that they found the right opportunity for their passion and talents, whether by serendipity or by actively looking for it. I expect that many opportunities excite you, and there is an abundance of innovation to be doing, so exploring those possibilities is exactly the right thing to do, but it's also important to feel free to let good ideas go in order to find the best opportunity for you—your purpose point. Then be sure to define the problem you want to solve with enough specification that you can craft a workable and distinctive model. Next consider the cultural shifts under way that you can capitalize on and be sure to build on your strengths. Also, find others to collaborate with or seek input from who have experience and talents that are not strengths of yours.

Though the myth of the lone founder who comes up with a brilliant idea and makes it work through the sheer force of personality and will has a powerful appeal, it's important to approach the building of your organization with humility. You *will* experience setbacks, there is no successful founder who will tell you he or she hasn't. Even the best ideas often need a good deal of revising, and it's vital to be open to input and acknowledge when you're stuck or have made a bad decision. Being humble in dealings with customers and employees also leads to a deeper connection and makes clear to them that you respect them and care about their needs and their ideas, which will strengthen their engagement with your mission.

Following the listen, build, and iterate method of developing your product or service ingrains humility into your design process, and it should be followed all the way through the creation of your organization and in each step as you proceed to grow. When you get feedback from the first couple of people you pitch your concept to, you have to be humble enough to internalize that feedback and be willing to rework, even quite substantially, whether that's with polishing your pitch deck, or in marketing testing of a prototype, or a year or two after launch when the model isn't working as planned.

Always be prepared to sell your idea and never underestimate how much hustling will be involved in getting it off the ground. The willingness to hustle was one of the most prominent features in the success of every one of the social innovators I interviewed for this book. They were relentless. But it's also important not to burn yourself out; you've got to protect your energy and time and make sure you are creating a sustainable pace of life so that you can be maximally effective. You're always going to have to be ready to hustle, but it's in the building phase that you'll be most intensely engaged in selling your vision and creating a support network, so be prepared that in this phase in particular, you're going to have to work some crazy hours and pull out all the stops. But to get as much control over the demands as you can and to increase output on your hustle, focus daily on a few essential things that you need to be doing. Also, know that even more hustle is always required when you are moving from one stage to another. So when you're heading into a next phase, take some extra time to relax, reflect, and recharge.

Chasing funding is one of the most time consuming and often frustrating parts of the hustle. Pitching to investors can be dispiriting, and writing grant proposals can suck the marrow from your bones, but always keep in mind that just one key investor coming onboard at the right time can make all the difference, and there are diverse funding sources to be tapping into. Be creative about options, and try out lots of ideas. Don't waste too much time pursuing funders who are wishy-washy. You want to be sure those who support you are truly in alignment with your mission, so it's best to move on and focus on those who are sure they want to commit.

Hustling means pushing hard to persuade and devising lots of angles to pursue, whether that's cold calling, email blasting, or staging an event, and it involves a good deal of salesmanship. But that in no way involves any lack of authenticity. People can spot a fake a mile away. It's vital for a social enterprise to be honest, not to be perfect. Talk about your failures and what you are doing to improve. That openness will be appreciated. And even when you're doing the hard sell, always be yourself and stay true to your authentic vision and purpose. Sincerity will go much farther than you might think.

Never, however, underestimate the power of some showmanship in your messaging and of creating delightful experiences for both your supporters and your end users. Always be thinking about drawing people into your story and how you can make it compelling and memorable, whether that's by being fun or unexpected, or whether that means offering some touch of especially thoughtful or personalized customer service or perhaps running a competition. Take advantage of all of the moments between moments to optimize every connection. You don't have to yell at your customers to get their attention; focus on delighting them instead.

As you get into the thick of building the organization, never lose sight of the rest of your team and of the larger community. Especially in rapid growth mode, it's easy to become almost entirely focused on all of the fires you're putting out and the grind of your own escalating volume of tasks to be keeping on top of, and the team and your community end up taking a backseat. Always make quality time to communicate with your team, and to engage with the community. You will build a much firmer structure for continued growth if you're sure to bring along an army of support.

Finally, be rigorous about evaluating how your model is working and creating honest, objective measures of your impact. In launching a social enterprise, we are holding ourselves to a higher standard, and it's important to be totally clear what that standard is and transparent about how well you are living up to it.

My hope is that this book inspires you to action. The future of the movement depends on more people becoming committed and bringing innovative ideas into it. I hope the stories in this book have inspired you and provided you with a set of insights and tools for going ahead and giving your idea a try. I also hope to cross paths with you at some point and hear your own founder's story.

Feel free to drop me a line and let me know how it's going at kyle@profit-purpose.com.

About the Website

This book includes a companion website containing a variety of resources to make it easy for you to adopt the principles of Profit & Purpose, including:

- Videos from top social entrepreneurs like Charity: Water, Burt's Bees, BUILD, and more, featuring pearls and pitfalls from the frontline
- Actual pitch decks used by social entrepreneurs to get funding
- How To worksheets: for example, how to crowd fund whether you are a for-profit or a not-for-profit entity

To access the site, go to www.wiley.com/go/profitandpurpose (password: wiley123).

Index